T0171616

Your Sacred Space

Your Sacred Space

A Guide To A Light-Filled Home

Alba Ambert

iUniverse, Inc.
Bloomington

Your Sacred Space
A Guide To A Light-Filled Home

English translation from the Spanish: Carleen Meléndez
Cover design: Yanira Ambert

iUniverse books may be ordered through booksellers or by contacting:

iUniverse
1663 Liberty Drive
Bloomington, IN 47403
www.iuniverse.com
1-800-Authors (1-800-288-4677)

ISBN: 978-1-4502-8675-6 (sc)
ISBN: 978-1-4502-8676-3 (e)

Printed in the United States of America

iUniverse rev. date: 05/04/2012

I dedicate this book to all spaces turning into Light.

In Appreciation

Heartfelt thanks to all who have generously used the teachings of the Paramita Path for the energy clearing of their homes, offices, institutions, public areas and other spaces. Their work has contributed to the healing of the Planet.

My deep gratitude to Vanessa Arroyo and Rafael Rivera for incorporating the material in this book in their work of Light. They have assisted so many people in transforming their homes and workplaces into sacred spaces. Many thanks to César Rivera for bringing his shamanic energy and love to public spaces. I am grateful to Carleen Zoë Meléndez for her sensitive translation from the Spanish version of this book and to Barbara Burman for her editing work.

I appreciate the beautiful cover and interior design work that Yanira Ambert always contributes to my books with love and generosity of spirit. To Walter McCann for opening the space of his heart.

To all who after reading this book put into practice space clearing processes, my deepest gratitude for the Light they bring into the world.

As always and forever, I thank the Creator for the Light of Divine Love that enlightens every step we take in this path of Love and Peace.

Contents

Your Sacred Space

Introduction

The Spaces Of My Life

From an early age I was fortunate to live in countless places throughout the world. The spaces of my childhood offered me a vast array of experiences in which I discovered that although there where spaces closed to love; most spaces remained open, generous, tender and willing to undergo transformations that would benefit the All. I discovered that in every space there is a sacred and permeable edge that when crossed allows us to become better people. In doing so, we transform the space and in a beautiful metamorphosis the space becomes an extension of ourselves. In all the spaces where I have lived, I experienced the full range of human emotions from deepest sadness to spiritual ecstasy. But most of all I was influenced by a subtle, ineffable energy that in my childhood I did not have the experience nor the vocabulary to describe.

I remember clearly how the spaces of my childhood offered a fertile ground for my imagination to leap and soar. When I was about eight my grandmother, who was my guardian, had a nervous breakdown and I ended up living with relatives in a modest room at a boarding house in the Bronx. Before World War II the brick structure was a luxurious residence, but with the economic and social changes of the postwar era the place had become temporary housing for those without the financial means to rent an apartment.

The decrepit boarding house maintained the solid mahogany furniture pieces that harkened to a prosperous past. Its corridors and stairways conserved the threadbare carpets that had seen better days. Upon entering the front door there was a large vestibule with a carved wooden vanity table leaning against a wall. The vanity had a round mirror stained by age and drawers on its sides with beautiful brass handles. A cushioned bench was in front of the mirror.

I sat in front of that mirror every day and, through the magic of the imagination, I transformed the ramshackle boarding house into a beautiful residence of happy people. While looking into that magical mirror, the ghetto became a golden city of light and the girl reflected in the mirror no longer wore clothes donated by the nuns of St. Luke's. Instead she became a beautiful woman attired in sumptuous gowns and sparkling jewels. Our room was on the third floor and when I ran upstairs, I imagined stepping not on scruffy carpets, but on the cushioned rugs of the Arabian nights. Soaring on the giddy heights of my imagination, I floated up those stairs like a queen.

That boarding house helped me escape the daily hardships of life, eased the pangs of want and allowed me to see possible worlds. I have no doubt that it was this space that revealed to me the vast powers of manifestation. Many years later and as a result of my husband's career in Europe, I attended the luxurious banquets I had imagined in my childhood at the time-stained vestibule mirror of the Bronx boardinghouse.

I will always be grateful to this and the other spaces that offered me so much.

My Work With Spaces

As I embarked on a spiritual path many years ago, it became clear to me that one of my missions was the energy clearing of spaces at very deep levels. After a transcendental spiritual experience that followed the dark night of the soul described so well by St. John of the Cross[1], I began a practice of meditation and prayer and sought guidance from the spiritual realms in finding my true spiritual calling. Almost immediately after requesting guidance, my hands became hot and I received the clear message that the portal to my spiritual evolution was through the healing of self and others.

So I began to search for a teacher and, as they say in spiritual circles, when you are ready your teacher will come. Mine was a sullen Englishman (at that time I resided in London) who occasionally ventured away from his healing sanctuary on the southeastern coast of England to teach in the city. Allan transmitted the attunements to open my energy systems so I could channel healing energy. He taught me many physical healing techniques. However, in his workshops

---

1   This experience is more fully described in my book *The Path of Light*.

Allan rarely mentioned the healing of physical spaces. On one occasion he shared with the workshop participants his experiences removing negative energies from spaces. But, he warned us, with a most solemn expression, to never attempt such work because we had to have a special gift to do so. And many years of experience were also needed. After listening to Allan talk about the daunting episodes he faced in his work with spaces, including dealing with perverse souls, I remember thinking that I was not at all interested in clearing spaces of negative energies and that my only desire was to work with universal energy, that is, positive, Light-filled energy. Soon I would realize that the Universe had other plans for me.

In London, I met several teachers devoted to the kind of mysterious work alluded to by Allan, yet none seemed to teach it. There appeared to be a secret society of practitioners who received instructions from a divine plane and were not allowed to share these esoteric teachings with others. But even when I heard about these teachers and the work that they did, I remained at the periphery this work that was considered to be so specialized and abstruse. For a long time I convinced myself that this work was not for me, yet deep down in my heart there was a restlessness that pulled me toward everything related to this area of spiritual practice and information reached me indirectly and in the strangest ways. Little did I know that the closely-guarded secrets of space clearing would one day be revealed to me in the most unexpected way.

Dennis was my teacher after Allan. I met Dennis through a Portuguese friend who invited spiritual teachers from around the world to her London home to give talks on topics such as Ashaya meditation, Tibetan mantras, spiritual healing and enlightenment. When I met him, Dennis was already an elderly man. He was tall, slim and his abundance of silvery-white hair reflected his quiet wisdom. His great devotion to the Virgin Mary led him to pilgrimages around the world where the Virgin's appearances were reported. He developed a healing system based on Marian energies and he offered attunements and teachings to individuals chosen based on their special devotion to Mary. He was a sweet, modest and profoundly wise man. I enjoyed listening to him talk about past lives and about his specialty, for which he was recognized all over England, of removing negative entities, lost souls, and other dense energies from homes and other spaces. So it was always comforting to think that if confronted with such a situation, I could always call Dennis or Allan and one of them would come to the rescue or at least know of someone who could do the necessary work. At no time did I ask myself why my first two healing teachers were "specialists" in space clearing. The reason I ignored it was because my mind did not want to accept the answer to something my heart already knew.

At that time my husband and I had an apartment in Puerto Rico. Every year during the Christmas season we traveled to the island from gray and rainy England to spend two or three weeks enjoying the sun and energizing warmth of the island. It was during one of those visits to Puerto Rico that I was driven, without warning, preparation or desire, to space clearing.

We were beset by an infestation of termites in several of the apartment doors, so we hired a carpenter named don Jesús to replace the doors. When don Jesús, a reticent, older man finished his work on the first day, he told us he would return the next day to replace the remaining infested doors. As soon as don Jesús left, I walked toward my bedroom, passing through the hall where he had been working for most of the day. Suddenly I was assailed by a terrible stench precisely at the spot where don Jesús had replaced a door. The hallway reeked of a combination of strong perspiration, urine, sewage and other foul odors I could not identify. I knew immediately what it was. I had read and heard about lost souls that stayed in places and caused difficulties. I realized too that don Jesús had brought them. And I didn't know what to do. Neither Allan nor Dennis had shared their knowledge on this subject with me. Being in Puerto Rico while they were in England did not offer me the option of calling on them for help. I knew immediately that it was no accident that this happened in Puerto Rico where I had no contacts with the esoteric world and that some way or another I faced an important lesson in my spiritual evolution.

So I sat at the edge of the bed and as I often do in times of need, I began to pray. I asked the Creator to help me. I prayed to Archangel Michael (since childhood I knew that he was the protector against all evil) and I asked my angels and other spiritual guides to give me guidance. As always happens when we reach out with an open heart and complete trust, Archangel Michael appeared in his sapphire blue regalia and guided me through it all. With his help and the assistance of all the beings of Light who came to guide the process, I managed to identify the seven lost souls that don Jesús unknowingly brought. Guided by Michael, I gave them the necessary assistance to go with the Light. Then I cleared the space energetically to harmonize any energy imbalance the souls may have created.

It was a fairly difficult process that first time. When it was over, I asked whether don Jesús had any more souls attached to him. I was dismayed to receive the message that he had five additional souls. The poor man, no wonder he was so sullen and never smiled. I was seriously tempted to telephone and urge him not to come just to avoid going through the same grueling experience. But I knew I had to help both don Jesús and the souls, so I got ready for another day of intense and unfamiliar experiences.

The following dusk don Jesús finished his work and, as expected, left behind the five remaining souls. Again, I was empowered in the process by the Light and led by Archangel Michael and other angels and beings of Light. With their assistance, the souls completed their transition and returned with the Light. Once the souls were gone, I energetically cleared the space, according to instructions, and for the first time I was able to relax into the realization of how beautiful this work is. I also knew without a doubt that I had to do this spiritual work and would always have the necessary support and help from the planes of Light to do so.

Over the years I have had to face difficult situations that I knew nothing about (at least at the mental level). This has been the way of my spiritual learning. I have been placed in situations that I have had to solve on my own by invoking the higher powers without having the option of calling a more knowledgeable or skilled person.

The experience with don Jesús' lost souls opened my heart to a Light that is different from the one I had accessed until then. By requesting and receiving the help needed in those difficult moments, I opened my heart to the generosity, kindness, compassion, confidence and great love that surround us. I call it Grace. I knew I would never be alone and that Grace, rather than a distant gift available only to saints and mystics, is as close to us as our heartbeat. Furthermore, I understood that there is no battle against negative forces. All we do in this work is bring the Light to illuminate the dark pockets of existence. At that moment of total surrender, with an open heart and complete confidence that help is there if I ask, my trust in the power of the Light bore fruit. In that moment of surrender, my heart declared to the Creator and to all the divine forces of Light that I would be present for whatever was needed, whenever it was needed. Waiting in a field of absolute Love, at that moment of absolute surrender, was Grace.

Not everyone has the task of clearing spaces as I was asked to do. However, all who desire to bring more Light into the world are tasked with working with their homes to transform them into sacred spaces capable of radiating Light at all times. Everyone can do this work. I have recounted the journey that led me to space clearing to reassure you that anything is possible when you have an open heart and complete trust in the Creator's Light.

In this book you will learn to work together with the spirits and devas of your home and to understand how your space interacts with universal energy. You will be shown ways in which you can cleanse, enhance and purify the energies of your home so it becomes a sanctuary for you, your family, friends and visitors.

I recommend that you read through the book first to get a good feel for the areas included and what is entailed in space-clearing work. When you read the book a second time, you will be ready to follow the steps involved in space clearing. Clearing and sanctifying space is a multifaceted process with many layers. This book is not as much a step-by-step manual as it is a tool box that gives you the necessary implements you will need to complete the process. However, the most important part of this work, and the main goal of the book, is to show you a simple way in which you can transform your home into a beacon of Light, a transmitting station of radiant energy that benefits everyone and everything on our Planet. You will learn to clear and enhance the energy of your space so it becomes a beautiful lantern beaming Light in these times of change for all existence. By transmitting Light, your home will draw even more Light toward itself.

Setting Your Intention

Intention is one of the most potent forces in the universe. When you set an intention, you are linked to a powerful universal force and everything that you intend to manifest, happens. Intention is one of the most effective human powers. Intention is magic. With intention you can desire a reality, create it at non-physical levels and then bring it into the physical world. Intention, simply defined, is the desire for something to happen or exist, fueled by the absolute certainty that it will happen. When you use this combination of desire and faith, miracles happen. We need to have the intention that what we want will happen, with absolute certainty that it will occur.

Intention is sacred and to prepare for the wonderful work of Light described in this book, it is helpful to set your intention. To derive maximum benefits, I recommend that before you start reading and performing the practices included in the book, you do the following meditation to open your heart and all of your energy channels so that your intention to transform your home into a sacred, Light-filled space manifests.

Meditation To Enhance Your Intention

1. Begin by taking a deep breath. As you breathe out, let go of all thoughts, all worries of the day.

2. Breathe deeply again and relax your body completely. By focusing on your breathing you are reminded of the peace and serenity that is in your being.

3. Feel your heart. Feel the infinite peace in your heart. This peace brings you to the present moment and when you are in the present, you are aware that you are peace.

4. Now, have the sacred intention that your home is a space devoted entirely to the Light and blessed by Divine Love.

5. Have the sacred intention that the space of your home opens up, like a beautiful flower, to give you the direction, motivation and knowledge you need to assist it.

6. Intend that your mind, your heart and your feelings absorb the information you receive from the planes of Light so you can transform your space into a sacred place of Light.

7. Have the intention to co-create a sacred space with the beings of the highest Light, the spirit and devas of your home and all the other nature spirits. This sacred space will be for the highest good of all who enter it and for the benefit of the entire planet.

8. Summon your spiritual guide and ask that all the necessary help be available to you and that you may be able to recognize it.

9. You can stay in this meditative state for as long as you like reflecting on your spiritual intention for the space and connecting with the Light that is within you and in your environment.

10. When you are ready to return from the meditative state, open your eyes gently and slowly, feeling a deep peace in your heart.

Energy clearing of spaces is spiritual work, a vital spiritual practice that benefits you, your family and everything and everyone around you. As you begin to do this work, intend to maintain a connection with the Light and make sure your consciousness is firmly placed in the present moment. Remaining in the present moment while you are conscious of your connection with the Light will help you to open your heart and remain linked with the spiritual planes while doing this work of Light.

1

The Sacred Space of Your Home

Home

Our home is a sanctuary where we long to return to each day. After the stress of work, rush-hour traffic, supermarket shopping or whatever else we engage in during the day; we yearn to return to a place that provides us with peace, protection from the energies of others, privacy and the comfort of silence. When we return home, after navigating the outside world, we cross a frontier into a space where we can escape the pressures of the daily grind. After we take off our shoes, bathe or wash our face to clear out the contaminants of the outer reality, our home offers us the pleasant relief of a perpetual return.

It is no wonder that the home is such a frequent theme in literature. A good example of an archetypal search for home is in Homer's *Odyssey*. Odysseus, the hero of this epic, is lost at sea and spends years overcoming arduous circumstances in his effort to return to his home on the island of Ithaca. It is the memory of his home, warm and full of love, which impels him to triumph over the treacherous sea, the monstrous Cyclops and overcome many other formidable adventures and temptations of all kinds, until he achieves his sweet return home. Just as Odysseus longed to be home, we also yearn for home; the space we always return to for comfort, rest, peace and a welcome sense of belonging.

It is this comfort, peace and calmness that a home provides which makes losing one's home such a devastating tragedy. The tragic loss of a person's special sanctuary occurs not only for the homeless. Domestic violence, where the home becomes an arena of abuse, and when the sacred refuge of a home is contaminated by the negative energies of others also constitute intolerable situations that create psychological, mental, emotional and spiritual havoc leaving us without a place of solace and rest.

Your home is more than a place where you are sheltered from the elements, where you retire to rest every night. Your home is more than a roof and walls. Your home is a place of infinite possibilities that can facilitate your connection with the Light and all creation. Your home can become a sacred beacon that radiates Light to the whole Planet. As such, it can become a transmitting station of Light.

Like waves that undulate on an infinite ocean, your home may transmit the radiant Light of divine Love everywhere. When your home is a sacred space, the Light it radiates can be felt at all levels of existence. The purpose of this book is to help you, with simple and specific techniques, to achieve this goal.

Sacred Spaces

We often believe that sacred spaces are located in remote and exclusive areas. We think that we can only access spiritual energies if we travel long distances to mountain peaks, mysterious geological formations or massive cathedrals built centuries ago. The ancient temple of Angkor Wat in Cambodia, built in honor of the Hindu god Vishnu, attracts visitors from around the world because of the many legends that proclaim its connection to the gods. Chichén Itza, one of the most famous architectural complexes built by the Mayas, is reputed to connect us with the cosmic memory of natural and stellar forces and the powers of beings from other dimensions. The ruins of Delphi in Greece, considered the center of the world, still retain the powerful energy of the ancient rituals that were practiced for centuries in its temples and altars. Another example of a place considered spiritually unique is Easter Island with its huge statues of magical emanations. Some experts consider it the center of the world with potent spiritual qualities.

All of these sacred places were consecrated and dedicated to rituals that brought practitioners to realms beyond the physical planes and into direct communication with the spiritual dimensions. During centuries of visits by people who opened their hearts to the possibility of connecting with gods, angels and other divine beings, sacred spaces around the planet accumulated vibrant energies that deeply moved those who came to their divine portals to be transformed.

The potential of these sacred spaces to connect people to the Light was true at a particular moment in the history of humanity. However, a vital transformation has occurred in the capacity of human beings to link with the divine planes. A new Light is flowing to the Earth now, making it possible for us to connect to very high spiritual planes. The powerful Light that is coming through has positioned us in a new era of spiritual evolution. As a result, sacred spaces are no longer found exclusively in places such as temples, churches and ancient monuments. As the new Light awakens our consciousness, our subtle energies become more refined and we can access the spiritual planes from the sacred spaces we create within us and around us.

Today we are in the dawn of an age of profound spiritual transformation as a result of major transformations in the Earth's energy. This is a new era in the evolution of humanity where a vital change has occurred in the capacity of humans to connect with the divine planes regardless of our physical location. Instead of traveling to churches and cathedrals to enjoy spiritualized energy, our mandate is to make each space on Earth a sacred space. A place whose energies vibrate at such a rapid and elevated frequency, they allow a drawing in and anchoring of the Light in its environment. Everyone in the world, without exception, can bring in and enjoy the Light. The divine Light is available to all. It is like the sun shining on every one of us without judging, without determining that only those who climb the steep steps of the pyramids of Giza or absorb the energies of the monoliths of Stonehenge may enjoy the sun. So it is with the Light. Whether we pray in the silent Cathedral of Chartres or at home in a quiet suburb of Miami, the Light illuminates us all. It is like drawing open the curtains or window blinds in our living room so that sunlight can enter. The same occurs with the Light. We just need to open our hearts and our space so that the radiant Light can enter and give us the beautiful gift of its Grace.

We are living at a time when an influx of potent Light is coming through to the Earth planes. This Light penetrates, saturates and activates. Its primary purpose is to transcend the density of the third dimension in which we live to lift the Planet and all her inhabitants into a new, highly spiritualized dimension of Light. This flood of Light transforms the Earth into a New World where everything and everyone, bathed in this Light, resides in our true space of Home and is One with our Divine Source. All this can be accomplished in our lifetime.

So at this unique stage in the history and evolution of humanity when the Light is helping us reach enlightenment en masse, it is no longer necessary to embark on long treks to the Ganges or to the Gothic cathedrals of Germany to receive the sacred Light in our hearts. Each of us can transform our home into a bright and beautiful sacred space and enjoy the flow of divine Light in our lives every moment of the day and night.

For this to occur it is important to connect to the Light with an open heart. It is also essential to be aware of our connection to Nature and to realize that we are part of everything that surrounds us. As such, we do the work of creating sacred spaces by co-creating with the spirits of nature and by working together with the consciousness of our home and all of the natural world around us. There are many beings in Nature that can and want to work with us.

Vibration

All space, including the space in your home, is a concentration of invisible activity and movement. The cosmic spheres, the galaxies, the earth, the molecules that make up your body; everything exists in a state of continuous pulsation. This movement of energy is called vibration. It is the vibration that exists in everything and everyone. While walking through your home or workplace, your body senses the subtle energy produced by this constant vibration.

The vibratory energy of atoms, molecules and subatomic particles has different patterns and frequencies. The frequency of vibrating energy or the frequency of vibrations is the rhythm and speed with which energy moves. A specific energy vibrates, that is, constantly moves, and this movement may have a different frequency from other energies. The movement may be faster or slower, depending on the specific energy that moves the object. For example, the frequency of vibration of a table is slower than the frequency of vibration of a glass of pure water. That is because the energies of the table have a slower rate, it is heavier than the energies of water. The higher the frequency of something, the higher its vibration and as the vibration is higher it is also less dense and lighter.

Spaces, then, are not empty places but areas of resonance whose energies are in constant motion vibrating at different frequencies. As discussed later, the energy and its vibration are affected by emotions, thoughts, words and intentions. The energy of a space is greatly affected and influenced by your energy and the energies of all persons associated with the space.

A space is composed of different vibrations that move to certain frequencies of oscillation or speed. The vibrations of the energy of a space can oscillate in a harmonious or unbalanced way. Spaces that vibrate at harmonious and high frequencies feel good, friendly and full of vitality. The energy is in a state of balance. But when a space vibrates at a frequency that is slow and unbalanced, the space feels dense, uninviting and may even seem like a dead space devoid of vital energy.

In summary, everything that exists is made up of energy that is in continual flux. Things that appear to be solid are actually composed of energy that is constantly changing. Your home is composed of this energy in constant flux, in perpetual movement.

The Light

The energy that underlies all space, all vibration, all creation is divine Love. This Love manifests as a beautiful Light that is always present, always at your disposal. Love is all that exists whether you call it Light or energy or movement. Love is the creative energy, the primary energy that gives life to everything and is composed entirely of divine Light. It is the creative impulse of the universe. All matter is created in, through and with Love. Love is the deepest reality of existence.

Light, the manifestation of Love, is the energy that causes the movement of atoms, impels life toward a greater evolution and radiates vitality at all times. Our bodies are created with Light, the energy flowing through space is Light and it gives life to everything that exists. The spaces we inhabit are also composed of Light. Everything in the universe and the whole of existence is constituted, formed and transformed by this Light.

You can, at any time, open your heart to the Light, the beautiful energy of Divine Love, and then radiate it to others and to the world. In the same way you can transform your home into a beacon that radiates Light to the world.

The Energy Channels Of Your Home

A number of energy channels form pathways throughout your home. These energy channels, known as the chakras, the sushumna and the meridians, process energy and allow positive, balanced energies to circulate and strengthen the space. Let us discuss the distinctive qualities of your home's energy channels.

Chakras

Just as your physical body has a series of chakras, energy vortexes that rotate and bring vital energy to your body, your home and other physical spaces have chakras too. Chakra is a Sanskrit word that means *wheel*. It refers to the energy center that serves as a transmitter or energy station drawing universal energy into itself and surrounding areas and pushing out the accumulation of unbalanced energy. Chakras process universal energy vitalizing the physical body. These energy centers also bring spiritual insight and assist in our spiritual evolution. They allow us to bring Light into our physical and energy bodies for spiritual growth.

Human beings have seven major chakras in their energy fields: (1) The root chakra, located at the base of the spine; (2) the sacral chakra, located in the pelvic area; (3) the navel chakra, in the abdominal area; (4) the heart chakra, at the chest and upper back areas; (5) the throat chakra, located in the throat and back of the neck; (6) the third eye chakra or ajna, located between the eyebrows; and (7) the crown chakra, at the top of the head. These centers of subtle energy are essential for our physical, mental and emotional well-being. Each chakra is connected to specific organs and glands and as they process the energy that flows into the body, they precipitate hormonal and cellular changes that balance our system.

In my work with spaces through the years, I have discovered that homes, apartments, work areas and other spaces with defined borders have five major chakras. These chakras are created with the combined energy of the space, the people who inhabit the space and the underlying Light that exists everywhere.

The five major chakras existing in spaces are:

- Root Chakra
- Creative Chakra
- Personality Chakra
- Heart Chakra
- Spiritual Chakra.

The following are the locations of your home's chakras and their qualities.

Major Space Chakras

Root Chakra

The root chakra is usually located in the kitchen or the place where food is stored and/or prepared. In spaces such as workplaces where there is no kitchen, the root chakra is situated in the area adjacent to the bathrooms. This chakra is the center of survival, nutrition and provides the energy necessary so we can feel safe, secure and confident that the world around us is benevolent and generous.

Creative Chakra

This chakra is located anywhere in the home where true creative thinking and other creative activities occur. It is the place where you tend to sit when painting, drawing, reading, or even when trying to think through a problem and find its solution. It may be located where the desk is or in a specific corner or nook of your residence where you tend to sit and think. This chakra provides us with the energy of creation that allows us to overcome external influences and create our own internal landscape: a landscape filled with peace and harmony.

Personality Chakra

Every house, apartment or workplace has its own personality. A space can be solid, reliable and secure. It may be light, happy and carefree. Or it may be dark, dense and uncomfortable. The personality chakra is an expression of the characteristics of a space and usually you can easily determine the personality of a space by walking through it and feeling its subtle energy. The personality chakra is not located in a specific place, although I have found that in most cases it is located near the heart chakra.

Heart Chakra

You may have noticed that there is an area of your home where people tend to naturally congregate. People enter through the door and, as if guided by a special radar, they head for that place. It can be the living room, dining room or another part of the space that feels warm and inviting. This is the place where the heart chakra of the home is located and it is very easy to recognize. The heart chakra, when not obstructed by negative energies, is a source of peace, love and joy. It is a harmonizing chakra that brings balance, healing and integration into the home.

Spiritual Chakra

The fifth chakra found in spaces, the spiritual chakra, is located at your home's ceiling. If you live in a house with several floors, the spiritual chakra is located at the ceiling of the top floor. If you live in an apartment building, there will be many spiritual chakras throughout the building since each apartment will have a spiritual chakra at its ceiling.

The spiritual chakra brings spiritualized energy of very high vibrations to your home. In our work creating a sacred space, the spiritual chakra assists us in bringing and anchoring the highest Light to the space.

The Sushumna

The sushumna is an energy channel that runs along the spine in humans. All major chakras are centered in the sushumna, running through the spine from the base, at the bottom of the backbone, to the crown of the head.

In physical spaces this essential energy channel runs through the center of the house or apartment from the kitchen or food preparation area to the front door. The sushumna in physical spaces is not a straight line, as in humans, but can wind through the apartment or house.

The chakras are connected to the space's sushumna through energy lines that extend from the core of each chakra to the sushumna. The purpose of the sushumna is to sustain the chakras in position and nurture their vital energy centers.

The Meridians

The meridians are the circulatory system of a space. Their energy lines run throughout the area bringing universal energy to nourish the space and, in a process of elimination, removing unbalanced energies.

When performing the energy clearing work described in this book, all the energy channels in the space are cleared, harmonized and all the energies are brought into balance.

The Home As A Living Being

Spaces are made of Light, the radiant expression of divine Love, so spaces have a life too. They have a spirit or a consciousness of being. Though different from humans, plants and other beings, your space is a living being with a consciousness that is specific to its particular life force. To be able to cleanse, harmonize, purify and heighten the energies of your home it is important to understand fully the living nature of your home. Your house or apartment has a soul, an aura and energy channels that affect it and allow it to bring the vital energy of the universe to its center. These energetic characteristics also allow it to radiate that vital energy outward. Because of its nature as a living being, you can communicate with your home and in this communication you can originate and maintain a strong connection between your soul and the soul of the space.

Your home is nourished by the love and respect you give it. When you understand and honor that it is a living being, your home can offer protection and healing to you and your family. Without this love and respect, your home becomes lifeless. It is wise to show the same reverence for our homes that we have for our bodies. Unfortunately there are too many instances in which homes have been reduced to inanimate objects rather than the vibrant beings that they truly are. When spaces are abandoned, ignored or treated with contempt or neglect their souls perish. They are incapable of transmitting the energies of vitality and joy that a healthy space is capable of doing.

Every home is an evolving being with its own personality. A home may be lively or serene, depressed or warm. Regardless of its personality you can help your home to evolve according to its destiny of Light. For this reason, it is important to respect your home and allow it to achieve its potential as you help it to harmonize and balance its energies. By focusing on the energy of the space and respecting its boundaries, we do not attempt to make the space change into something that it is not. Rather, we attempt to harmonize and balance what is already present. If the space exudes a happy and lively energy, for example, it is best to avoid trying to turn it into a quiet room and dim its energies. We accept the joy and vitality of the space as something that already is, and with the specific energy practices discussed in this book, we optimize the capacity of the space to fulfill its highest potential. In this way, when a happy and lively space has its energies harmonized and balanced, its negative energies removed and the space spiritualized; the space's vivacity is transformed into an energy of expansive and deep joy.

Your Space And You

An important factor that determines the success of your work with spaces is the recognition that your home is not a being separate from you, just as you are not separate from the world around you. All is one including plants, minerals and animals. Everything in creation is part of All-That-Is and your home is also one with you. In addition, everything that exists has a consciousness that affects what is around it. Therefore, your home reflects your own state of consciousness.

In summary, to work effectively with spaces, you need to:

- Be aware that your home is energy and this energy is the Light, the manifestation of divine Love.
- Recognize that your home is a living and evolving being with its own consciousness.
- Accept that your home is not an entity separate from you; it is one with you.

When you connect with your home at deep levels, respecting the space by recognizing it as a living being and understanding that it is one with you, you can create a balanced life that is in harmony with everything around you. As you recognize that your home is a living being, you can communicate with it. Your home loves you and wants to help and take care of you. It can evolve as you evolve. So in your work with spaces you are not only focusing on what you can do for your space, but also what your space can offer you. A balanced and harmonious space has the potential to offer its residents healing and serenity. With a deep understanding of the interconnectedness between you and your space, it is easier to clear, purify and raise the vibrations of your home and transform it into a true beacon of Light.

Our Spiritual Allies

As you begin the process of transforming your home into a sacred space, remember that you are not alone. The spiritual planes of Light are filled with angels, archangels and other beings of the highest Light who are willing to help you at all times. According to spiritual laws, these beings of Light must always respect your free will. Therefore, if you would like their help you must ask for it. When you do the processes in this book, you will work cooperatively with these beings of Light so that everything you do is completely spiritualized and in harmony with the highest Light. You will also work with the spirit of your home, the protective spirit of your home and with the devas of your home and land.

The Spirit Of Your Home

All space that is contained within borders and boundaries such as a house, an apartment, a workshop or an office, has a spirit. Your home has a spirit that has within itself the consciousness of your space. It communicates with you and can help you perform energy clearing and maintenance with its positive energy and disposition. You might see, sense or perceive the spirit of the home as a fairy or an angel or simply as a being of Light. The spirit of the home may be perceived differently by each person depending on his or her expectations.

The Deva Of Your Home

Your home also has a deva[2]. *Deva* is a Sanskrit word that means "brilliant being." Devas are beings of the natural

---

2   A more detailed description of the devic world appears in my book *Your Sacred Apothecary.*

world that serve as intermediaries between the physical and spiritual realms. They are expressions of the divine impulse of creation through which the essence of Light is transmitted to a specific form of earth energy for a specific purpose. Devas offer the world the energies that allow it to evolve according to its nature. For example, the deva of the rose transmits the necessary energies for each rose to bloom with the colors, scents and other characteristics of its unique rose nature.

Devas specialize in different tasks. There are devas who work with flowers, shrubs or trees. There are devas whose functions include supplying vital energy to mountains and there are devas dedicated to the balanced functioning of closed spaces such as houses, apartments and other residences. There are also devas in charge of the energetic lines and grids around the Earth. The land where your home is located also has a spirit and a deva who function within this external space.

The Spirit Protector Of Your Home

Every home has at least one protective spirit. But, there may be more than one. It can be an angel or a legion of angels. It can be a dragon or an army of dragons. A dragon and an angel can combine their energies to be the protective spirit of your home. Any combination is possible, including animal guides as in Native American traditions, or Hindu deities such as Ganesh or Shiva. All you need to do is to think of a being of Light who you feel is close to you and who you usually invoke when needed.

When you complete the process of transforming your home into a sacred space, you will perform a ceremony in which you invoke the spirit protector you have chosen for your home and ask that, with great respect and love, it protect the sacred space of your home and all those living in the space and all the people who enter the home. The energy, Light and unconditional Love of this protective spirit will always be present protecting the sacred space in its entirety.

To reaffirm your connection with the spirit protector, it is a good idea to place an image of the being or an object that symbolizes the spirit protector at the main entrance, door or gate of your home. For example, you can use the symbol of OM, or a simple silver circle, or the painting of a rose and place it at the door with the intention that the image represent the protective spirit of your home.

At the entrance of Chinese and Japanese temples there are often gigantic dragons carved in stone because in Asian cultures the dragon is considered to be a divine protector. The gargoyles that adorn the exterior of medieval cathedrals focus their gaze on all those who pass through the entrance, protecting the sacred space from negative influences. According to Native Americans, every human being has their own guardian spirit, called a power animal. If you feel your spirit protector is the spirit of a power animal such as a wolf, a hawk or a dolphin, you can invoke it.

However, the most recognized protective beings in our culture are angels. From our guardian angel, the personal protector who warns us of impending dangers, to Archangel Michael, whom we see or perceive with his sword and shield at times of major negative onslaught, angels are the beings of Light who are closest to humans and most willing to help us in all our pursuits.

Angels

The term *angel* means messenger of God and certainly angels bring us continuous messages from the spiritual planes. Angels are pure beings of Light sent to the world to ease our journey on the physical plane. Angels are divine beings of the highest Light and not the souls of family members who have made their transition and passed on to the other side.

If we ask, angels can help us in any aspect of our lives. They respect our free will, but when we ask for their help they provide assistance with unconditional love, compassion, and without judgment. They recognize that we are sparks of the Divine and it is with this divine aspect of our being that they communicate. Their motivation is to help us achieve our greatest good. They do so with pure, generous and kind love.

From birth you are accompanied by a personal guardian angel that is always at your side. Not all angels are guardians. Other angels may come to help you when you ask for assistance. It is possible to have more than one angel helping you. These angels will continuously protect and guide you. You just need to listen to them.

If you want to have more than one guardian angel accompanying you, enter a meditative state and within the silence of your heart ask that more angels be sent to you. Visualize the angels surrounding you and you will see how in a very short time you will have all the guardian angels you want.

Archangels

Archangels are divine beings of Light, like the angels mentioned above, but who have broader responsibilities than angels. Like the angels, they have no gender so that when we speak of Archangel Michael using the male pronoun, for example, this is only our own projection. Archangel Michael —as all the angels, archangels and other beings of Light— is an infinite composite of beings of Light with certain specific energies and these energies are neither masculine nor feminine, but tend to have energetic qualities that humans identify as female or male.

While there are many archangels, the descriptions that follow will only include some of the archangels who have volunteered to work at the Temples of Light of the Paramita Path. The Temples of Light are spiritual temples, each with its specific angelic custodian, that exist in the Earth's energy field. The purpose of these Temples is to assist us in our spiritual evolution. In our sleep or during profound meditative states, we can travel to these temples to receive guidance, increase our vibrations and attain higher states of consciousness, bringing our higher consciousness back to the physical world. In my extensive work over the years with the angelic realms I have received and continue to receive information on the missions of archangels and the specific purposes of the Temples of Light. The information has been communicated directly by the beings of Light themselves during deep states of meditation.

Archangel Michael

In the experience narrated in the introduction of this book, it was Archangel Michael who showed me the way when I did my first space clearing work. When my spiritual teachers in the physical planes were reluctant, for protective reasons perhaps, to offer the necessary training for my mission on this planet, it was Archangel Michael and his angels of protection and purification who gave me the step-by-step lessons needed to do this work of Light. Not only did Archangel Michael show me clearly the necessary techniques, he also armed me with the courage and determination I needed to work with darker energies. Archangel Michael is the custodian of the Temple of Delos, the spiritual temple for work that entails the dissolution of negative energies, protection, purification and bringing Light where there is darkness.

Archangel Michael doesn't always capture my attention when I'm meditating or praying. Since I have been known to spend several hours a day on the computer, especially when writing a book, he has been compelled at times to use unorthodox ways to convey urgent messages that could not wait for my daily meditation sessions. One afternoon, I opened a program on the computer and in a flash that lasted maybe a second, enough for my senses to perceive it, the message "Contact Michael" flashed on the screen. You can imagine how quickly I left the office and sat down on my cushion to meditate and allow the urgent message from Michael to come through my awareness. Indeed, I received his message and quickly realized that urgent work was needed to dissolve harmful negative energies that would have caused much damage to someone.

Currently, my mystical states are not dependent on designated meditation sessions, so Archangel Michael does not need to communicate through my computer. He just gives me a nudge.

The name Michael means "he who is like God." Archangel Michael is a powerful protector against evil in all its manifestations. He has a keen sense of justice and a fervent mission to protect everyone who walks on the path of Light. He is the protector of the innocent.

I've seen him dressed in sapphire blue, a great and powerful being, with a Roman-style sword and shield. Underlying his commanding strength and power is a gentle current of unconditional love, compassion and kindness. Archangel Michael holds a huge golden sphere of Light. We can enter this sphere and bring our spaces into it to dissolve negative energies more effectively.

It is not accurate to say that Michael slays the dragon. The dragon has been misidentified in Christianity as a demonic being. However, the dragon is really a being of Light with energies that are very similar to Archangel Michael's. The dragon's purpose is to protect the Light and its mission is the dissolution of evil. As such, Archangel Michael is accompanied by a beautiful Golden Dragon to help clear negative energy and bring purification to the world. The Golden Dragon is a being of the highest Light. He assumes the form of a dragon to better annihilate the powers of the negative forces. The angels of protection and purification also assist in this work of dissolution of negativity.

Archangel Gabriel

Gabriel means "messenger of God" and this archangel brings us the fundamental message of divine love and the request that we love others as God loves us. Archangel Gabriel radiates an energy of divine love that is powerful and delicate at the same time. The love that he transmits is charged with subtle and countless frequencies that communicate to us the infinite ways in which the Creator loves us and the multitude of ways in which that Love is expressed for everything and everyone.

Archangel Gabriel assists us in our mission to love and heal the Earth, animals and all other beings of nature; helping lost souls to go with the Light and helping people at the time of their passing and newborns at the moment of birth. Archangel Gabriel also assists us, with his energies of pure love, to heal our karma and access our Akashic Records where we may attune to universal wisdom. In the Temple of Culebra, where Archangel Gabriel dwells, one of the most beloved bodhisattvas of compassion, Avaloketishvara, assists him in this work.

Archangel Raphael

His name means "he who heals" and as his name indicates Archangel Raphael is the compassionate spirit of healing and regeneration. I have always seen him dressed in purple robes, holding in his right hand a wand-shaped quartz that radiates a laser-sharp healing light and his left hand holds a vessel that contains the essence of all crystals, flowers, trees and medicinal herbs.

Archangel Raphael offers comfort, tenderness and compassion punctuated by unfathomable love. He holds the suffering of the sick and transmutes it into Light at deep energetic and cellular levels. In many cases those involved in Paramita Path[3] group healings have seen him placing the person receiving healing on a beautiful quartz healing table and kneading the Light into the person's cells, organs, tissues, glands until the person shimmers with the healing radiance of the Light.

---

3   The Paramita Path is a spiritual path dedicated to union with the Divine Presence and service to all beings. For more information on the Paramita Path please see Appendix III.

Archangel Raphael also seals the chakras of those receiving healing so that nothing negative can penetrate them, only the Love and Light of the Creator. Working with Archangel Raphael at Temple of Victoria are the Medicine Buddha and the Angels of Healing.

Archangel Uriel

Her name means "God is Light." This archangel has broad roles that extend into many realms. She is the custodian of the Earth for the purpose of helping the planet reach its destiny of Light. As such, she helps us raise the vibrations of the planet and works with us to heal the grid surrounding the Earth. As the Earth is healed, so are all of Her inhabitants including the animal, vegetable and mineral kingdoms.

All meditations done for the Earth and invoking Archangel Uriel will have a positive impact in bringing divine Light more deeply into all levels, all dimensions, all alternate realities, all spaces, all times that exist on Earth. Within this space of Light, we co-create a new world of beauty, peace, harmony and love. We co-create a spiritualized and enlightened world. We can intend to travel to the Temple of Light to work with Archangel Uriel in healing the Earth.

Archangel Zadkiel

Archangel Zadkiel is the spirit of forgiveness, tolerance and mercy. Like all angelic beings his love for humanity is unconditional. In Archangel Zadkiel this Love is laced with the soothing elements of tenderness and compassion. This archangel represents the essence of tenderness and compassion. He assists those experiencing desperate situations and who need healing, warmth and comfort. He also assists those who exploit and otherwise inflict pain on others and this assistance is offered with unconditional love, compassion, tolerance, mercy, forgiveness and without judgment. Many beings of Light work with Archangel Zadkiel at the Temple of the Himalayas, including Mother Mary and Kuan Yin.

The Angels Of Karma

Karma is a Sanskrit word that means *action* and it refers to the Universal Law of Cause and Effect. According to this Law anything that we do, think, say or feel has an inevitable consequence and this consequence can be positive or negative, depending on the nature of our actions, thoughts, words and emotions. Karma is accumulated throughout our lifetimes and it has an impact on all aspects of our present lifetime. By transmuting negative karma into positive karma we are able to liberate our soul from the unnecessary suffering of endless reincarnation. The Angels of Karma are very high spiritual beings that work with us to heal and dissolve karma. Dissolving karmic blockages, negative interference of karmic origin and general karmic healing are essential when we clear spaces. In this way, the space we work on is free of burdens originating in the past lives of its spirit, deva and other spirit beings that may exist within it. For this reason, in some of the sacred space processes you will be requesting karmic healing for different purposes.

The spiritual allies mentioned help us to gain a better understanding of the Light and to be aware of the infinite number of beings of Light who help us at all times. In the meditations and processes included in this book, you will invoke the presence of these beings of Light who always help us in a loving and tender way. With their assistance, our work becomes easier, broader in scope and complete. As we work we are harbored in a protective sheathe of Light.

2

Basic Steps of Space Transformation

As you set your intention to transform your home into a sacred space, you deepen your understanding of your home as a conscious being, with a spirit and deva who will work with you throughout the process. You realize that there are also many spiritual allies willing to work with you. All you need to do is ask. Space transformation is a beautiful, spiritual practice that enhances the lives of those who embark upon this heart-opening experience and you will find, as you work through the basic steps of space transformation that just as your space is transformed, you are transformed as well.

The basic steps to transform your home into a sacred space are as follows. In subsequent chapters we will describe fully each step:

1. Preparation
2. Communication
3. Diagnosis
4. Physical cleaning
5. Energy clearing
6. Geopathic stress curing
7. Transformation
8. Maintenance

1. Preparation

Before you begin working on your space, prepare yourself for the task ahead of you. Preparation includes protecting your energy channels so that no negative energy affects you, invoking the assistance of the beings of Light and removing any impurities that may prevent you from accomplishing your spiritual work in an exalted and graceful way. Proper readiness involves preparing yourself at physical, mental, emotional and spiritual levels to undertake the venture that you intend with the proper respect and devotion to the Light.

2. Communication

The next preparatory step is to communicate with the space with love and respect in order to recognize it as a conscious being that is one with you and to capture the idiosyncrasies of its personality. As you do this, you are better able to understand the needs of the space and how you can provide it with the necessary assistance.

By communicating with the space, you also communicate with the spirit and deva of the space. This enables you to work with them in a co-creative attitude, manifesting the ideal transformations for the space, nature and all existence.

3. Diagnosis

The third preparatory step involves diagnosing those areas of the space that require energy balancing so it can achieve a state of harmony in its being. For this purpose, you apply specific techniques to detect the subtle energies of the space and its condition. Diagnosis involves observation and energy scanning. These are essential aspects in communicating with your space.

The identification of unstable, dense, unbalanced and stagnant energies will help you bring these energies into perfect balance.

4. Physical Cleaning

After the diagnosis, you clean the space physically. Negative energies that are caused by lack of cleanliness, clutter and general disorganization are easy to remove. Physical cleaning greatly facilitates the energy clearing work that follows since it eliminates many of the negative energies in the space. This simplifies energy clearing work and brings a sense of lightness to the space.

5. Energy Clearing

When the space is physically clean and free of clutter, you clear the space energetically. This involves invoking beings of the highest Light to help you, seeking the help of the spirit and deva of your home and performing specific tasks that facilitate the removal of unbalanced energies. Once this process is done, the energy of the space regains its natural harmony and achieves a balance that brings peace and lightness to the area.

6. Geopathic Stress Curing

Any energy clearing needs to include curing geopathic stress in the space and its environment. Geopathic stress is a complex condition created by negative energies in the Earth's energy channels that form intricate grids throughout the globe. Contamination of these grids can cause various health problems, instability, mental and emotional problems and general disharmony in a space and in its residents.

7. Transformation

Once your home is clean –physically and energetically– its energies balanced and in harmony, you follow specific steps to transform it into a sacred space. This ritual of deep transformation and spirituality is a beautiful experience and it will bring a lasting peace to your life. You will have made possible the transformation of your space into a beacon of Light for the world.

8. Maintenance

Finally, you will want to maintain the sacred space you have created so that it continues radiating Light to you, your family and the world. To maintain your sacred space, it is helpful to ensure that its energy is always balanced, harmonious and constantly bringing in the Light that it can radiate to its surroundings. By using the elemental energies, sound, quartzes, colors and many other of the techniques suggested in this book; you will be able to maintain your sacred space free of negative energies.

3

Preparation

A universal element of most spiritual practices is proper preparation before proceeding. From the simple act of making the sign of the cross upon entering a Catholic church or washing the feet at the entrance of a mosque, to the more complex preparatory practices of full body bathing in the Ganges as the Hindus do, preparation rituals are intended to remove negative energies and purify both the physical and energetic bodies before participating in spiritual ceremonies.

But purification is not all. A spiritual practice requires a particular state of being that demonstrates respect and devotion to the divine Light and the beings of Light who help us. We also need to raise our vibration sufficiently to move to the spiritual realms with ease. Creating a sacred space is an elevated spiritual practice. As such, it requires proper preparation at the physical, mental, emotional and spiritual levels.

Physical Preparation

On the morning when you plan to clear your space, begin by bathing or taking a shower to cleanse your physical body. If you bathe in a tub, place several tablespoons of sea salt in the bathtub with the intention that the salt removes all negative energy from your physical body. A few drops of an essential oil such as lavender or frankincense in the water will strengthen the purification process. If you take a shower, rub your body with sea salt and intend that when you rinse, all the negative energy in your physical body will completely dissolve with the water[4].

Once your physical body is cleansed wear clean, light-colored clothes. Avoid wearing red or black clothes since black tends to attract fear and red is a stimulant that may hinder your efforts to bring peace and serenity to the space. If possible, refrain from wearing jewelry. Gems tend to collect negative energies and when you finish the energy clearing of the space, you will need to clear the jewelry to remove the negativity adhered during your work.

Mental Preparation

At all times before and during this work, be prepared mentally for the process you are about to undertake. Breathe deeply and have the intention of silencing your thoughts. Try not to think about the things you have to do later or the things that are worrying you at the moment and that have nothing to do with the space. It is important that you remain in the present moment, focused on the task at hand. The quickest way of being

---

4   See Appendix II for more information on the aromatherapy products Ezencia that include bath salts specifically created to dissolve negativity and for protection.

in the present moment, without the interference of thoughts or emotions, is feeling the divine presence in your heart and letting the divine presence bring you to the present.

Another technique to mentally prepare yourself is to make several affirmations that can help you stay focused on the work you are doing. Remember that for affirmations to be effective, they must be stated in the present tense and contain only positive words. Some affirmations that you may want to use are:

My space is sacred and dedicated entirely to the Light.
My space is radiant with Light and it brings balance and harmony to my being.
Peace reigns forever in my space.

Once you are fully in the present moment, take a few minutes to reflect on the space clearing you are about to undertake and the importance of this work for you, your loved ones and for the benefit of the entire Planet.

Emotional Preparation

Take a deep breath before beginning and as you exhale let go of all thoughts and any concerns you might have. Feel the center of your being, that core of your being that brings a feeling of balance, of equilibrium to your heart. This center is the essence of your being where you connect with the infinite Light.

Feel this center, this core of your being. You need not make any effort in feeling it. Let your heart guide you until you can sense it. Just move into your heart and allow a feeling of relaxation, balance and harmony to flow through you. Feel that you are connected to your essential being and feel the infinite peace that exists there. It is while feeling this peace that you will be able to easily and gracefully transform your home into a sacred space.

Spiritual Preparation

Spiritual preparation entails assuming a neutral attitude toward the work to be done. This means that we do the work with an open heart, conscious of the spiritual importance of our task, but surrendering the results to Divine Will. Thus, we do not become attached to the results. On the contrary, we have absolute trust that everything will be done for the highest good. As we step away from our emotions, expectations and attempts to control the process; we allow the Light to flow freely through us transforming, with its splendor, our space and ourselves. The following is a meditation that will assist you in surrendering all the processes you will be doing to Divine Will.

Meditation To Surrender The Sacred Space
Processes To Divine Will

1. Take a deep breath and relax your body completely.
2. Invoke the presence of the angels, archangels and other beings of Light. Ask for their guidance as you prepare yourself to do this work of Light. Ask that they assist and protect you so that everything flows according to Divine Will.

3. Intend to be conscious at all times that it is not you who is doing this work, it is not you who does anything. You are a simple instrument of divine Light and Love. Intend that   Divine Love flows through you and your surroundings in all of its splendor. Intend that everyone in existence can feel the divine Light and can feel the infinite Love that blesses the world.

4. Intend to aside your ego and allow all of the words, thoughts and actions that flow from inside you to be inspired by divine Light.

5. Intend that within you there be no trace of arrogance, of feeling spiritually superior to others, of feeling that you know more than others.

6. Instead of these ego-generated emotions, intend to feel the purity of Light in your heart so that this purity dissolves everything that is not Love within you.

7. Intend that, with the help of the Light, the only things that can exist in your heart are Love, Light, peace, tenderness and infinite compassion toward everyone and everything.

8. Have the intention of radiating Love and Light at all times during this work of Light that you are about to do.

9. In this sacred moment, surrender completely to the Light so that the Divine Will be done on this day and every instant of your life.

10. End your meditation by thanking all the angels, archangels and beings of Light who help, protect and accompany you always.

In addition to surrendering the sacred space processes to Divine Will, it is recommended that before you begin any type of spiritual work you protect your energy channels including your aura and chakras. This protection is especially important when engaging in energy clearing that involves the removal of unbalanced energy, a common situation in space clearing. By taking the necessary precautions described in this book, all negative energy present in the space can be dissolved easily with the Light so it does not penetrate your energy channels. If you follow the processes outlined here, you will not run any risk of contamination with negative energies, since you will be fully protected and all negativity will be transmuted into Light.

The following meditation will help raise the vibrations of your physical and energy bodies and bring you into harmony with the Light. In addition, your heightened vibrations will protect you from the impact that any dense energy in your space might have.

Meditation For Protection

1. Start by breathing deeply and when you exhale, let go of all thoughts, all worries of the day.

2. Take another deep breath and let your body relax completely.

3. Now, feel your heart. Feel a deep peace settling into your heart.

4. And feel how the purity of Divine Light flows through you.

5. Empty yourself out of everything else and let the Light fill your entire being with its beauty and radiance.

6. Feel the luminous and radiant Light flowing through and around you. You are radiant with the Light.

7. Your body becomes a permeable membrane. All the Light around you flows through you and the Light in you radiates out to your surroundings.

8. Continue to feel this flow of Light until you dissolve in the Light.

9. You and the Light are one. Dissolve, dissolve completely in the Light.

10. A radiant sphere of Light forms around your aura. The angels and other beings of Light bring more Light to your aura and this Light protects you completely.

11. You are completely protected and empowered by the Light. Feel how radiant and luminous you are now with the beautiful Light you have, with the radiant Light that you are.

12. You can stay in this meditative state for as long as you like reflecting on your spiritual intention for the space and connecting with the Light that is within you and in your environment.

13. When you are ready to return from the meditative state, open your eyes gently and slowly, feeling a deep peace in your heart.

Attunement

Spiritual preparation to create sacred spaces includes surrendering all the processes to the Divine Presence and the protection of your aura and other energy channels so that dense energies will not affect you. After these preparations, there is one important preparation that needs to be done. It consists of receiving an attunement to activate and open your energy channels so you may channel Light through them. An attunement is a spiritual ceremony in which you connect to the Light and harmonize your energy with the Light's energy patterns so the Light can be used for spiritual work. In addition to harmonizing your energy with the Light, in the attunement you open your energy channels to receive the Light more effectively, thereby enabling you to be an instrument of the Light in your spiritual processes.

Your Energy Body

Besides your physical body, you have an energy body composed of the aura, chakras and other subtle energy systems that are similar to your circulatory, nervous and lymphatic systems except that because they are purely energetic they cannot be seen with the physical eyes. These energy centers and channels that course through your body and radiate energy well beyond your physical body, allow for the vital energy of the universe –what we call Light– to flow and power your physical body with the vital force it needs to survive. The chakras are energy centers located throughout the body. They rotate continuously bringing pure energy into your body and extracting negative energy. We have seven major chakras in our energy body. The main chakras are connected to the sushumna, our main energy channel located in the spine. The chakras connect to the sushumna and they run vertically from the base of the spine to the crown of the head. The sushumna and chakras form an energy processing system that brings nurturing Light into our bodies and spirit and extracts denser energies.

The Seven Major Chakras

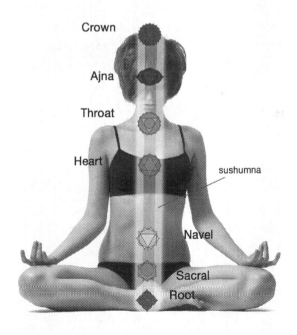

Crown

Ajna

Throat

Heart

sushumna

Navel

Sacral

Root

(Root chakra is located at base of the spine)

In addition to the major chakras, we have hundreds of minor chakras throughout the body, including small chakras at the palms of the hands. In order to perform the processes indicated in this book, it is necessary to open and activate your crown, heart and palm chakras. This allows the Light, which is the universal energy that gives life to everything, to flow through your body, coursing down through your crown chakra, to your heart chakra and, from there, flowing through the energy channels in your arms to pass through the chakras at the palms of your hands. The Light is everywhere. All we need to do is open our energy channels to receive it.

In the following meditation, you will receive an attunement to open and activate your crown chakra, heart chakra and the chakras in the palms of your hands. Your energy will be harmonized with the energy of the Light. By only having the intention to do so, you will be able to activate the process by which you bring Light to your energy channels and then radiate it through your hands. After the attunement, you will practice feeling the Light flowing through your hands and you will learn how to radiate the Light. This step is essential for you to be able to do the processes in this book.

During the attunement, you receive the ability to transmit the divine energy of Light. This transmission is bestowed upon you from the highest planes of Light and all you have to do is have the intention of receiving the attunement. It is a spiritual gift of great value given to all who open their hearts to divine Grace. In the attunement, a special link is created between you and the divine energy of the Light so that you can radiate this Light for spiritual purposes.

To summarize, in this attunement you connect to and harmonize with the energy of divine Light. Once you receive the attunement, all you need is to have the intention of radiating Light and you will be able to absorb the energy of divine Light through your crown chakra and bring it to your heart and through your arms to the chakras at the palms of your hands. You will then be able to radiate Light in your spiritual work with spaces.

As you work with these energies, you will be more conscious and have a deeper perception of what you feel and see. Your sensitivity to subtle energies will increase every time you radiate. You will also experience changes in yourself as you become more balanced and develop more self-confidence.

As you do the following attunement meditation, feel in your heart the great gift of Grace that you are receiving and be deeply grateful for this opportunity. The Light will flow through you and when this happens there is no distinction between your being and the Light that flows through you. You become a part of this beautiful blessing of Light. Dissolve in the blessing. Allow yourself to be completely in the moment. Forget your ego, forget your personality. Let go of all your expectations, thoughts and fears. Simply be. Before you begin, light a candle and incense. If you have an altar, do the attunement meditation in front of your altar.

Attunement Meditation To Open The Chakras And Radiate Light[5]

1. Sit comfortably, with a straight back and your hands on your lap, palms facing upward.
2. Begin by breathing deeply and as you exhale, let go of all thoughts, all worries of the day.
3. Take another deep breath and allow your body to relax completely.
4. Now, feel your heart. Feel a deep peace settling into your heart.
5. And feel the purity of the Light flowing through you.
6. Empty yourself out of everything else and allow the Light to fill your whole being with its beauty and radiance.
7. Feel the radiant and luminous Light flowing through you and your surroundings. You are radiant with Light.
8. All the Light around you flows into you and the Light in you flows into your surroundings. Continue feeling

---

5   Attunement meditations, practices to perceive energy, to radiate and to make a Chi Ball are included in this book for the benefit of those who have not taken the Paramita Path workshop *Creating Your Sacred Space* and only need to be done once. If you have taken the workshop and received the attunements, you do not need to do the attunement meditation or the practices to perceive energy, radiate and make Chi balls. However, if you wish to strengthen the attunements and practices, you may repeat them as often as you wish.

this flow of Light until your body dissolves in the Light.

9. You and the Light are One. Dissolve, dissolve completely in the Light.

10. Now, feel how the Light flows into your crown chakra, located at the top of your head.

11. The Light activates your crown chakra and your crown chakra begins to spin counterclockwise and then clockwise. (Pause for a few minutes while the crown chakra activates.)

12. Now feel how the Light continues to flow through your crown chakra and your crown chakra opens and fills with Light. (Pause for a few minutes while your crown chakra opens.)

13. Your crown chakra is active, open, radiant and filled with Light.

14. Now, feel the Light flowing down from your crown chakra and filling your heart chakra, located at the center of your chest.

15. The Light activates your heart chakra and your heart chakra begins to spin counterclockwise and then clockwise. (Pause for a few minutes while the heart chakra activates.)

16. Now feel how the Light continues to flow through your heart chakra and your heart chakra opens and fills with Light. (Pause for a few minutes while your heart chakra opens.)

17. Your heart chakra is active, open, radiant and filled with Light.

18. There are energy channels that transport the Light through your arms to your palm chakras. Feel how the

Light flows from your heart chakra to your shoulders and through your arms. The Light then continues flowing from your arms into your hands and fills your palm chakras.

19. Feel how the Light activates your palm chakras and your palm chakras begin to spin counterclockwise and then clockwise. (Pause for a few minutes while your palm chakras activate.)

20. Now feel how the Light continues to flow through your palm chakras and your palm chakras open and fill with Light. (Pause for a few minutes while your palm chakras open.)

21. Your palm chakras are active, open, radiant and filled with Light.

22. Feel the Light now, flowing down through your crown chakra to your heart chakra and flowing down your arms to the palms of your hands. You might feel warmth, tingling or some other sensation in your hands.

23. Enjoy the Light that is flowing through you for a few minutes.

24. When you are ready, return from the attunement meditation. Thank all the angels, archangels and other beings of Light who helped you and open your eyes slowly and gently.

Practice To Sense The Energy

A good way to start sensing the energy of the Light between your hands is by doing the following practice:

1. Sit in a comfortable position and take several deep breaths.

2. Hold your hands up to chest height with the palms facing each other and the width of your body between them. Let the hands relax so that the fingers separate naturally. Notice what you sense.

3. Bring your hands together slowly, noticing any sensation.

4. Now, hold the palms of your hands facing forward and intend to radiate Light. Wait until you feel the energy flowing through your palm chakras. You may feel warmth, tingling or other sensations as the energy flows.

5. Hold the palms facing each other again at about the width of your body. Feel the energy between your palms now.

6. Bring the palms together slowly and feel the sensations in your hands. You may have sensed the energies as a soft ball between your hands or you may have felt a magnetic charge as you tried to bring your hands together.

7. As you do this several times, you will find that you are more sensitive to the energies and can perceive them better every time.

Practice To Radiate Light

Radiating the energy of the Light is easy. You simply have the intention that the Light flow through you. The Light is all around you. All you need to do is intend to open yourself to receive the Light and it will be there, flowing through you. Once you feel the energy between your hands in the previous practice, you can begin to radiate as follows:

1. Sit comfortably in a chair, with your back straight. Do not cross your legs as this will interfere with the flow of the Light. Close your eyes.

2. Hold your hands, palms facing upward, in a relaxed manner. Now, have the intention of radiating the energy of divine Light.

3. With intention only, the energy will begin to flow automatically. You might feel a sensation of warmth or pulsation in the palms of your hands.

4. When you feel the energy flowing, place your hands on your chest. Observe the sensations. Do you feel that the palms of your hands become warmer? Or do you feel a pulsation? Do you feel any other sensation in your chest? In your hands?

5. Place the palms of your hands facing upward again and feel the sensations in your hands.

6. Place your hands on your chest again and hold them there for several minutes.

7. Continue this practice until you can feel some sensation in your hands.

8. If you don't feel anything, don't worry. With practice and as your energy channels become more sensitive to the subtle energies, you will begin to feel the Light you are radiating. Even if you don't feel it, the Light will flow through you the moment you have the intention of radiating the Light.

Chi Ball

Once you have received the attunement and practiced radiating Light through your hands, you are ready for the next step in the process of spiritual preparation. You will now learn how to make a Chi Ball. The energy globe called a Chi Ball has been used effectively in many healing traditions to store energy and use it for different purposes, such as healing, increasing the energy in the body, for protection and to clear negative energies, among many others. *Chi* is the vital energy that exists in all things. It is another name for the radiant Light that enlivens everything including our physical bodies.

Now that you have been attuned to bring the energy of the Light to your chakras, you can easily store this energy by preparing a Chi ball in the process that follows.

Process To Prepare A Chi Ball

1. Hold your hands in front of you about 12" apart with palms facing each other, as if you were holding an invisible basketball.

2. Intend for the Light to flow down and visualize that you are molding an invisible ball of Light by physically moving your hands slightly towards each other and then back. Continue moving your hands back and forth gently as you form the ball.

3. As you feel the ball of Light between your hands grow, continue to work with the Chi Ball. Notice the

sensations your body is experiencing as you work with the Light.

4. Continue holding the Chi Ball and let it fill with Light.

5. When you feel that the Chi Ball is dense and well-formed, have the intention of placing yourself inside the Chi Ball for protection from any negative energy contained in the space you are working with. Simply visualize yourself inside the ball and surrounded by protective Light.

6. Once you have visualized yourself inside the Chi ball, in your heart express the intention of being completely protected by the Light.

7. When you are finished, let go of the Chi ball gently.

The Temple Of Light

When the Paramita Path came to this Earth to help us reach enlightenment, we were given the beautiful gift of spiritual temples that would facilitate our spiritual journey. Each temple has specific purposes. In the advanced Paramita Path workshop, you receive information about all the temples.

Space clearing, as practiced in the Paramita Path, is done from the Temple of Light, a spiritual (etheric) temple that exists to help us bring in and sustain the Light in the physical planes. From the Temple of Light we invoke the presence and assistance of Archangels Gabriel and Michael. We also invoke the presence and help of the angels of protection and purification and other beings of the highest Light.

Before doing a space clearing for the first time, you will need to receive an attunement to open a path of Light that will allow you to journey directly to the Temple of Light easily and safely. This attunement, transmitted directly by one of the Paramita Path teachers during the workshop *Creating Your Sacred Space*[6], ensures that the gates of the Temple of Light open for you. During the attunement a special energy is transmitted that facilitates your journey to the Temple of Light so you can work from there.

If you have not attended the workshop, you can do the following attunement meditation so that a path of Light opens and brings you directly to the Temple. Once you have received the attunement, every time you have the intention of going to the Temple of Light, you will arrive there and no where else. All spiritual work done from this Temple has great power and an energy of Love that is highly spiritualized. Before you begin the attunement meditation, light a candle and some incense. If you have an altar, do the attunement meditation in front of your altar.

---

6   *Creating Your Sacred Space*, levels 1 and II, are advanced Paramita Path workshops. For more information on these and other workshops, please see Appendix III.

Attunement Meditation To Enter The Temple Of Light

1. Begin by taking a deep breath. As you breathe out, feel your body relaxing completely.
2. Breathe deeply once more and let go of all thoughts, all worries of the day.
3. When you are completely relaxed, feel your heart.
4. Feel the Light in your heart.
5. Your heart is a radiant beacon of Light. Enjoy the Light in your heart for a few moments.
6. There is so much Light around you now. Enjoy the beauty of the Light.
7. The Light flows into your brain cells and your pineal gland, awakening your intuition and giving you the ability to perceive the Light in all of its manifestations.
8. The Light flows to your third eye chakra, like a beacon. Everything in you and around you is filled with crystalline clarity.
9. Feel the Light within you and in your surroundings.
10. Feel your chakras. Your chakras are centers of radiant Light.
11. Feel how open and radiant your chakras are now, glowing beautifully.
12. There is a sphere of Light around your aura. This sphere of Light protects you completely.
13. The angels, archangels and other beings of the highest Light bring more Light into your sphere. You are completely protected by the Light.

14. Now, invoke the presence of Archangels Gabriel and Michael and the angels of protection and purification. When you feel their presence, with your heart open and filled with love, ask them to open a path of Light to the Temple of Light and to open the gates of the Temple of Light so that you can enter and do the sacred space work there.

15. Once you have made the above requests, wait in a meditative state until you feel or sense or perceive that a path of Light is cleared to the Temple of Light and that the gates of the Temple are open. This process may take from three to five minutes.

16. When you feel that the gates to the Temple are open, with intention enter into the interior of the Temple of Light and feel the energies of pure Love that are there. Enjoy the energies of pure Love that exist in this Temple for a few minutes.

17. When you are ready to return, thank Archangels Gabriel and Michael and the angels of protection and purification for their loving assistance.

18. Return to the physical planes with deep gratitude in your heart for the blessings received.

Once you have completed the prayers, attunements, meditations and practices in this chapter, you have the necessary energetic and spiritual preparation and protection to continue with the work that will transform your home into a sacred space.

4

Communication

Optimal communication with your home is facilitated by your understanding that a space is not like a person. Rather, it is helpful to perceive the space as a living being **equal to** a person. These two concepts are different and it is useful to recognize the distinction.

As we move from a self-centered vision –where we see ourselves reflected in everything– toward a broader perspective of nature, we recognize that everything in Creation including spaces, plants, animals, rocks and all else that exists, are conscious, living beings. We recognize that we relate to and interact with each other as one. It is not that the space is like a person but that the space, just the same as a person, is a living being that senses and is conscious.

By communicating with the space, you honor it. A good first step to initiate this communication is by walking through the space with the intention of understanding it. While doing so, imagine that you are looking at your house or apartment for the first time. The following process can help you to communicate effectively with your space.

Process to Communicate With Your Home

Stand at the front door and have the intention of communicating with your home. Begin to feel the energy that emanates from your space. If you find it easier, close your eyes to deepen your awareness of the space's energy.

Now, look at the front door. What impression does it give you? Is it warm or does it seem to want to keep people out? Do you feel that your home welcomes visitors? Do you feel that it welcomes you and the other residents of your space?

When you enter, how do you feel in the space? Is there a place reserved for shoes, for example, indicating that those who enter are coming into a special space?

How does the space smell? Does it smell musty? Is there a dank smell or the smell of deterioration? Is there a bad smell? Are there any odors you cannot define? Or does it smell good?

What general impression does your home give? Does it feel cozy, serene, sterile, dense, disorganized?

Close your eyes again and ask your home how it feels. In your heart sense whether the space is unhappy or depressed, happy or sad, angry or satisfied.

Ask your space if it has something to communicate to you and remain silent until you receive a response. Have a notebook handy so you can record the messages received before you forget.

Now focus your attention on the energy of the space. How do you sense the energy? Is it an energy that invites you to stay or is it an energy that encourages you to leave as soon as possible? Does it feel dense or light? Is it a comforting or off-putting space?

With your hands outstretched, go around the house or apartment feeling the energies of each room. Are there areas in the space that feel stuck, where the energy is not moving? Use your hands like radars to detect areas of dense energy.

Now, stand in the center of your home and feel the energies of the whole space.

Does it feel like a happy place, a space that nourishes your soul (or the souls of those who live there) providing a sense of wellbeing? Or do you feel a dense atmosphere, heavy and lacking joie de vivre?

As you open the channels of communication with your home, you establish an intimate relationship with the space, feeling its soul and the many ways in which it manifests.

5

Diagnosis

The diagnostic process is one of the most significant elements in the energy clearing of a space. To greatly facilitate the energy clearing work and to accomplish your goal in transforming your home into a sacred space, it is essential to determine the areas that need clearing, the unbalanced elements in the home and how to identify them. At the end of this chapter you will find a questionnaire that will help you determine the scope and extent of negative energy in your home.

People are affected by thoughts, words and negative actions. So are spaces and even water. Dr. Masaru Emoto is a Japanese scientist who has demonstrated in impressive photographs the negative effects of words, thoughts and emotions on water molecules[7]. Dr. Emoto's research confirms what was already

---

7   Dr. Emoto's books include impressive photographs that document his research.

obvious to many: that thoughts, emotions and words have an energy that affects people, animals, things and spaces. When negative situations occur in a place such as violence, harmful exchange of words, negative intentions and emotions and other adverse situations, the negative energy generated permeates the space, unbalances its energies and distorts it. The area becomes a "sick" space. Just like human beings, spaces can suffer from ailments that deprive them of the balance and harmony that naturally exists within them.

I will always remember one of the first spaces I cleared some weeks after my experience with don Jesús' lost souls. Isis was a young housewife who was quite distressed because despite having done everything possible to bring positive energy into her home, there was still a bedroom in the house that seemed impossible to clear. Although Feng Shui techniques had worked in the rest of the house, which felt quite light and airy, none of the specialists she had consulted had been able to help with the room.

The situation had reached the point where no one in the family wanted to be in that particular room and when guests visited and stayed in the bedroom overnight, they invariably became ill. Isis was in an advanced stage of pregnancy and needed the room for her newborn. But she knew intuitively that because of the energetic conditions of the space, it was not appropriate for a baby.

As soon as I entered the bedroom, the dense energy almost knocked me over. When I scanned the space, my hands became sticky prompting me to ask Isis if something negative had happened there. She replied that her husband's grandfather, who was a grumpy, extremely negative person, had suffered from a long illness and died in that room. It was no wonder that the room still had an imprint of pain that was palpable. The room held within its energies the negative emotions, illness and fears of the person who had died there. When I finished clearing the space, the energy in the room harmonized with the energies of the rest of the house. Isis was able to prepare the room for the boy she delivered shortly afterwards.

To diagnose the energy of your space, you will utilize methods of observation and scanning. Observation is the systematic registering of events to obtain pertinent information. Scanning is an action that is done by feeling sensations with your hands to verify if there are any unbalanced energies in a space.

Observations

As you perform the diagnostic process, think about the situations, events and incidents that have occurred in the space. For example, whether someone in the home is experiencing or has experienced a chronic illness or whether frequent arguments occur in the space. If so, identify the location within the house or apartment where the illnesses or arguments have occurred. Observe the places where things tend to accumulate, where there are messes or clutter. Make a note of the areas of the house or apartment that are usually empty because residents or visitors avoid being there. Also note whether there is a room where someone has suffered a long illness and/or passed away.

Scanning

Before you begin to scan the space, place your hands in the "Namaste" position (or prayer position) at your forehead, thumbs lightly touching your third eye chakra located between your eyebrows[8]. With eyes closed, ask the beings of the highest Light that are helping you to guide you to those places that require energy cleansing at a deep level.

After asking for guidance, place your hands in front of you, palms facing upward, with the intention that the Light flow through your hands so you may be able to identify those areas in the space that require energy clearing. Then, slowly move through the house or apartment while scanning the space with the palms of your hands facing forward at the level of your chest. Remember to scan the energy in corners, under furniture (especially under beds), inside closets, inside cupboards and in other dark places where negative energy tends to accumulate.

As you walk through your home using your hands as scanning devices, identify specific places where the energy feels strong, negative or stagnant. Negative energy can be defined as energy that is unbalanced, dense and unharmonious.

You may feel some sensations in your hands when you come across unbalanced energy. The sensations may include tingling or a feeling of pins-and-needles in the palms of your hands. You might even feel sensations in other parts of your body, such as tingling or itching in your scalp. Your hands may become hot or cold. Or you may feel stickiness in the palms of your hands. Any unpleasant or unusual sensations in your hands or other parts of your body are an indication of unbalanced energies that need to be cleared and harmonized.

Levels Of Unbalanced Energy

As you scan the space for unbalanced or dense energies, you can determine the level of density by the sensations in your

---

8   Touching this chakra activates your internal vision so you may receive spiritual information.

hands. Keep in mind that you might feel these sensations in other parts of your body, such as the back of the neck, the scalp or the legs. The following is a scale to help you determine the severity of unbalanced energy in the spaces you scan. The scale is from 1 to 5. Level 1 is the weakest level and level 5 represents the most severe.

1. The heat in your hands is higher than body temperature.
2. Intense heat. Your hands sweat from the heat.
3. You feel tingling, pins-and-needles, itchiness, a magnetic feeling or numbness in your hands.
4. Pulsation, coldness or stickiness. The pulsation can be strong or weak, slow or rapid. At this level you may also feel stickiness or a cold sensation in your hands.
5. You feel pain. The pain can be felt in the hands, fingers or the backs of your hands. Sometimes the pain can rise through your arms to the elbows and rarely, all the way up to the shoulders. The pain may be felt in one hand or both.

When you scan, make a mental note of the specific places where you feel stagnant or dense energies. These places may be corners or rooms where people do not like to be in, spots that emit a sensation of lifelessness or are areas where there appears to be a lack of energy, a lack of vitality.

Don't forget to scan items such as artwork, decorations, curtains and objects that may have been given to you as gifts. The objects need to be scanned to determine if they have unbalanced energies. Above all, make sure to scan items such as antiques, used furniture and other used articles that you may have inherited. Items that belonged to other people will carry their energies and may need to be cleared.

Artwork

Paintings, sculptures, pottery and other works of art are infused with the energies, thoughts, emotions and intentions of the artists who create them. If an artist or artisan is in a negative emotional state such as anger, depression, bitterness, hatred –or if she or he is sustaining negative thoughts such as revenge, suicide or negative intent toward another person– these negative energies will saturate the work that is created. This is why when we view a work of art we can be emotionally affected by the energy of the work.

Once I was invited to offer a workshop at a healing center. When I walked into the workshop area, the energy felt dense and quite negative. Although the area had been cleared energetically that morning, the negative energy was still evident. When we scanned the space we identified the cause of the density. A series of paintings were hanging from several walls and they emitted an energy that was extremely unbalanced. Once the paintings were cleared energetically, the space acquired a wonderful lightness and clarity and the workshop flowed smoothly.

Antiques And Used Objects

When you buy antique furniture, vintage clothing or any other used object, make sure you clear it energetically before bringing it into your home. If you have already brought a used object home without clearing it first, scan the object and clear its energy following the process described in this book. Our energy imprint permeates all the things we own and the objects in our environment. This includes furniture, clothing, jewelry and even the walls. When we purchase or inherit an object that has belonged to someone else, this object is saturated with the energies of the person who owned it and these energies will affect us and have an impact on the space we inhabit. For this reason it is important that when you scan your home to identify the areas that need clearing, you also scan objects that belonged to others and energetically clear them to keep their energies from contaminating the spaces of your home.

Caroline is a young medical student who called me because for several weeks she had been feeling ill every time she went into her bedroom. She had been experiencing insomnia and when she did sleep, her dreams were very dark and disturbing.

I asked her if she had brought something into her bedroom recently that had not been there before the onset of her sleep disturbances. After thinking about it for a moment, Caroline revealed that at about the time when she had started to feel unwell, she had bought a cedar chest at a used furniture store. The chest was in her bedroom. As soon as the chest was energetically cleared, Caroline felt that the energy in her bedroom became lighter. She was able to sleep normally and her nightmares became a thing of the past.

Questionnaire To Diagnose
Negative Areas

✓ Are there ants or other insects in the space? If so, where?

✓ Are there mice or rats?

✓ Are there any plumbing problems in the space?

✓ Are there frequent power outages or mechanical failures?

✓ Does the computer and/or internet connection have frequent breakdowns or other problems?

✓ Are there frequent problems with electrical appliances?

✓ Are there cracks in the walls of the house, apartment or workplace?

✓ Where do you feel stuck energy?

✓ Where does clutter tend to accumulate?

✓ Which closets contain the things you try to avoid, such as things that you never use yet keep hidden in a closet because you cannot part with them?

✓ Is there any specific place where plants wither or die?

✓ Do any of the residents experience insomnia and/or frequent nightmares?

✓ Do any of the residents have a chronic illness? If so, did the illness begin when they moved into the space?

✓ Does anyone living in the space suffer from depression or constant tiredness? If so, did these health problems begin when they moved into the space?

✓ Do these persons feel better when they are somewhere else?

✓ Are there any persons in the household who feel uncomfortable, anxious and nervous about the "atmosphere" of the space?

✓ If so, in what areas of the home do people feel uncomfortable, anxious or nervous?

✓ Did someone who previously lived in the house or apartment suffer from any long term or serious illness?

✓ Has there been any construction work near your home? Or any landslides, road works or broken mains?

✓ Does the home or any part of it feel too cold or humid?

✓ Is there "dead", stagnant energy or a low level of vitality in the space?

✓ Are there places in the space where arguments or fights tend to occur?

✓ Has there been a divorce while inhabiting this space?

✓ Has anyone died in the space?

✓ Is there a cemetery or a funeral home nearby?

✓ Is there a hospital nearby?

✓ Are there frequent car accidents on nearby streets?

6

Physical Cleaning

Before clearing your home energetically, it is recommended that you do a thorough physical cleaning of the space. Removing clutter and physically cleaning the space are essential preparatory steps to energy clearing. If while scanning your home you notice the presence of clutter, messiness or general lack of physical cleanliness, these factors will have a substantial impact on the energies of the apartment or home and they will generate dense and even stagnant energy.

Unwholesome blockages can occur in areas where there is disorder, lack of cleanliness and clutter. It is similar to an arterial blockage that impedes the blood from flowing into the heart. In the same way, a home suffers an obstruction of the energy flow when an accumulation of things clutter its spaces. The vital energy that nourishes the space is blocked and cannot flow properly, creating sluggishness in the energy. This sluggishness depletes the space of vitality and warmth. When the energy has been stagnant for long, it becomes negative energy and is more difficult to dissolve. The importance of recognizing the effects of clutter, messiness and lack of cleanliness in a space cannot be emphasized enough. Clutter and messiness may be evident not only in open spaces, but also in closets, drawers and other enclosed areas.

Before clearing the space energetically and particularly before performing the sacred space process, it is necessary to clean the space and eliminate clutter bringing the space to a physically clean and neat state. If a home is unclean or cluttered, both energy clearing and the sacred space process will be ineffective since harmonized energy and the Light that is brought into the space cannot remain for long in a disharmonious place. The best way of ensuring that a space can be effectively transformed into a sacred space is by eliminating the clutter and cleaning up any dusty and soiled areas first.

Physical cleaning –like vacuuming, mopping and dusting furniture– need not be a boring or unpleasant chore. You can bring the act of physical cleaning to a higher level by transforming it into a spiritual discipline.

Cleaning As A Spiritual Discipline

The physical cleaning of your home can become an effective spiritual practice. It is not helpful to face your cleaning tasks with a negative attitude, feeling bored or impatient. This only helps to create more negative energy in the space. The most beneficial attitude when faced with the chore of cleaning a space is to feel joy and peace in anticipation of a job well done. By using your cleaning tasks as a spiritual discipline, you derive the benefits of doing your spiritual practice while you clean and at the same time you transmit positive and harmonizing energies to the space you are cleaning.

In many religions cleaning is considered an act of respect and reverence toward the Divine. Members of a Christian sect known as the Shakers considered physical work, especially cleaning, as a way to give God a necessary offering. In Bali people sweep their balconies and the sidewalks around their homes every evening. They perform this practice rhythmically and with great care because they are performing a ritual of purification of the space, removing the negativity accumulated during the day by sweeping it away.

Dissolution Of The Ego

Eliminating clutter, discarding gifts that hold negative energies, giving away items to which we are attached, can be performed as exercises to dissolve the ego. Every time you discard something you own, you get rid of attachments that tie you to the material world. By giving away clothes that you do not use, you let go of ideas that you have about yourself. For example, you may have the idea that you are a person who uses a certain type of clothing. But that is not who you are since your core being extends way beyond what you wear. So when you let go of clothes, you can do it purposefully letting go of the idea you have about yourself and you work on the dissolution of your ego.

The past is one of the favorite places of the ego. As a spiritual discipline, the physical cleaning of your home is a good way to release the past and all the emotions attached to it. When we get rid of old magazines, old photos, old letters and damaged or worn objects we let go of the past, an essential step in the dissolution of the ego.

The physical cleaning of a space is an opportunity to practice the cleaning of your shadow self. This is a very important spiritual discipline that contributes greatly to the dissolution of the ego. The shadow self is comprised of those aspects of your personality that you deny, that you do not recognize as present in you, but when you identify them in other people you react very strongly to these characteristics or behaviors. For example, you get angry when someone does not listen to you, but you fail to recognize the many times when you don't listen to what other people tell you because you are too distracted thinking about something else. Yet you have convinced yourself that you are a good listener

So as you clean, don't focus on the tediousness of scrubbing the floor while you wish you were doing something else. Instead, just imagine that you are scrubbing away an aspect of your shadow self that you would like to dissolve, such as anger, impatience or judgment.

Physical cleaning is a powerful chore to help you tackle other ego issues. Let's say you feel pride because something went well at work. You give yourself a little too much credit and you notice some arrogance rising within you. Scrubbing the oven or the floor helps you to return to reality, it helps you to ground yourself in the core of your being and realize that this feeling of pride is not something you want inside you. With intention, you scrub away the pride and replace it with love, compassion, peace and joy.

Physical Cleaning As Meditation

As you physically clean your space, just imagine that it is a form of meditation. Focus on what you are doing and do it with serenity and joy. Let the rhythm of the broom when you sweep the floor or the rhythm of the hand that polishes the tabletop bring you to the present moment. Don't think about other things while you clean, but take the opportunity to be in your heart, feeling a deep peace in your being. You can chant a mantra or repeat affirmations while you work to help you focus on the present moment. Be aware of the rhythm of each movement and as you scrub the oven or the sink, have the intention of scrubbing away all emotions, all fears, all the worries that take you out of your heart.

When you consider that physical cleaning is a spiritual discipline, it becomes a more practical and even enjoyable task. As you realize that you sweep away outdated thoughts, fixed beliefs, rigid ideas; and that the emotions that bring you so much pain fade with the dust that you clear away; then physical cleaning becomes a practice that assists you on your spiritual journey.

Criteria For Cleaning

As you clean your home, keep in mind the following criteria that can help you discard items you no longer need. To bring simplicity to your life, you may want to discard the following:

- ✓ Clothes you have not worn in a year.
- ✓ Clothes that are no longer in fashion.
- ✓ Clothing that does not fit you, is stained or torn.
- ✓ Clothing or items purchased on impulse that you have never worn or used.
- ✓ Whatever you do not use in the kitchen, like pans that have lost their non-stick coating, dishes and other items that are chipped, cracked or broken.

✓ Canned or frozen foods that are past their expiration date.

✓ Cosmetics that you have not used in a year.

✓ Expired medications.

✓ Old papers you no longer need, such as expired car registration documents and old insurance records.

✓ Books that you have read and know you will never read again.

✓ Magazines that are over a year old.

✓ Unnecessary photos.

✓ Videos and DVDs of movies you saw and do not plan to see again.

✓ CDs that you no longer listen to.

✓ Letters and email received over a year before.

✓ Gifts you dislike.

✓ Items you inherited from your parents or other relatives that you do not use or like.

✓ Gifts that you have received from people with negative energies.

Recycle papers and magazines; donate books, CDs and movies to a public or school library. Donate clothing and gifts to charitable institutions. If you have items of sentimental family value that you do not wish to keep, offer them to a family member who will appreciate them. Throw away everything else.

If an employee cleans your home, this may have an impact on the energies of the space and it is something you will want to consider in this work. If the cleaning person does not respect the space, does the cleaning reluctantly, feels resentment or bitterness toward his/her employer, this will affect the energies of the home. Ideally, when the physical cleaning is done before the energy clearing, the owner or tenant of the house or apartment should do it.

7

Energy Clearing

Harmonizing Your Space

Energy clearing of spaces is a spiritual practice in which we align, harmonize, purify and elevate the energies of an area to help it achieve the highest possible vibrations and attain its destiny of Light. This requires that stuck, unbalanced energy become harmonized and aligned. Just as our physical bodies can become ill, spaces can get sick as well and one of the purposes of energy clearing is to heal the spaces that need it.

One of the reasons why this work is so important is that humanity has lost its ability to exist in harmony with its environment. We need to remember that in the depths of our hearts we are one with everything and we have a responsibility to undo all the damage that has been done to the Earth by recovering our gift, our ability to co-exist and co-create with nature and with universal energy. We start this process by energetically clearing our space. By performing this labor of love and kindness, we become conscious that all is One.

As you practice the steps described in this book, you can recover your innate gift to connect with nature. You discover that you can effect essential transformations in your home and your environment so that the Planet may return to her naturally high vibratory state that is Light-filled and stable. In this process you clear the space energetically while at the same time you raise its vibration, harmonize its energy and transform it into a sacred space for the benefit of the Planet and all her inhabitants.

Benefits

The advantages of clearing old and stagnant energies are many. You can anticipate that all aspects of your life will benefit as a result of space clearing sessions. These clearings enhance your physical, emotional, mental and spiritual life. Even plants grow healthier in a home with harmonized energy. The relationship and communication among the people living in the space also improve. After a space clearing session, you can feel the lightness that results from the fresh flow of vital energy in the environment and this new flow can even help improve the financial situation of the residents and brings to them a feeling of prosperity, peace, harmony and joy.

I remember the case of Mariana who came to see me some years ago. She and her husband Charlie were about to divorce after 17 years of marriage. The beautiful house they had bought several years earlier had become a battlefield. The couple fought constantly and, since they had no children, they were both able to spend as much time as possible at work to avoid coming home. When Mariana consulted me about her case, I suspected that there were energy problems in the home since almost all of the couple's arguments originated in the bedroom.

Indeed, when I visited the space I found a very dense negative energy in the master bedroom, especially near the bed. I asked Mariana if she knew who had previously lived in the house and she said that the couple who had sold them the house divorced after the wife fell in the bedroom and broke her back. After the accident she was bound to a wheelchair. Once the divorce was final, the husband moved out of the house and the woman died shortly afterwards.

A deep energy clearing was performed. The clearing included helping the soul of the paralyzed woman to return with the Light. After that space clearing, Mariana and Charlie stopped fighting and what surprised them most was that Mariana became pregnant some months later. They now have a beautiful daughter.

Although the specific benefits mentioned are extremely important for the welfare of those living in a space, the most significant blessing that results from this work is that the energy field of your home can be transformed into a beacon of Light for the good of the Earth and all her inhabitants. When your home receives constant energy from the forces of Light around it, the space can then radiate its own Light outwards creating a resonating field of radiant Light that affects all its surroundings.

So after clearing and harmonizing its energies, your home can serve as a gathering point of Light and a transmitting station radiating the Light everywhere.

Specifically, energy clearing has the following benefits:

- Increased energy and vitality of those who live in the space.
- Improved quality of sleep.
- Strengthening of the immune system.
- Fewer physical illnesses.
- Improved communications.
- Improved relationships among those who live in the space.
- Fewer insects in the space.
- Healthier and more peaceful pets.
- Enhanced creativity.
- Improved financial conditions.
- More birds and butterflies in the environment.
- Healthier plants.
- A sense of peace, prosperity and harmony.

Ethical Considerations

The process described in this book is for personal application in your home or workplace. If you would like to clear a space that is not yours, you need to request permission from the owner or tenant of the house, apartment, land, office or factory[9]. It is important at all times to behave ethically when working with the energy of others. It is not permissible to do energy clearing of your mother-in-law's space, for example, because you think it is for her benefit and do so without her permission while she is out of the country on vacation. Always ask for permission.

---

9   Working on another person's space is not recommended until you have acquired ample experience working on your own space. In the advanced workshop, *Creating Your Sacred Space II*, you will receive the necessary training to work on spaces that belong to others.

Your Tools

To perform an effective energy clearing, you may want to have the following items on hand. You can prepare a fabric bag or straw basket to hold these items so that your work tools are ready when you need them. In describing the process later in this chapter, we will indicate how to use these tools.

List of Tools

- ✓ *Room Clearing* mist by Ezencia[10] or a sage stick
- ✓ Lighter or matches
- ✓ Pendulum

Energy Space Clearing: The Steps

- **Preparation**. Take the necessary preparatory steps, as indicated in previous chapters. After the appropriate preparation at the physical, mental, emotional and spiritual levels, you will be ready for space clearing.

- **Prayer**. Say the following simple prayer and invocation that covers these points: You request assistance in becoming an instrument of divine Light. Then, you fill yourself with Light and with intent form a sphere of radiant Light around your aura for protection. In the third part of the prayer, you ask to be taken to the Temple of Light along with the space you will be clearing and you invoke the presence and support of the angels, archangels and other Beings of Light to help you.

---

10   *Room Clearing* is a spray by Ezencia that combines the essential oils of plants that are effective in dissolving negative energies. In Appendix II you will find more information on Ezencia products.

Prayer And Invocation Before Energy Clearing

I request divine assistance, blessings and protection during the space clearing of my home.

I am grateful for this opportunity to be an instrument of the Light to bring balance, cleaning, harmony, transmutation of energy and purification to this space.

I surrender my ego, my desires to want to achieve something specific so that divine Light may move through me and the situation for the highest good of all.

I am grateful for the assistance of all the beings of Light that are always here to help me.

I surrender the fruits of this work because it is through the power of the Light that this work is done.

Now, have the intention of placing yourself in a Chi Ball for protection. When you feel that the Chi Ball is formed and you are inside it, continue with the prayer:

I intend to go to the Temple of Light along with the space I am working on.

When you feel or sense that you are in the Temple of Light, make the following invocation:

I invoke the presence and assistance of Archangel Gabriel to help me in this work.

When you feel or sense the presence of Archangel Gabriel make the following invocation:

I invoke the presence and assistance of Archangel Michael and the angels of protection and purification to help me in this work.

When you feel or sense the presence of Archangel Michael and the angels of protection and purification, make the following invocation:

I invoke the presence of the spirit and the deva of this space and I intend to work with them at all times for the highest good of the space and all living beings.
I intend that this work harmonize, balance and bring peace and Love to this space and to all its inhabitants.

After finishing the prayer and invocations, you are fully protected. You and the space you are working with are in the Temple of Light with the angels, archangels and other beings of Light you have invoked.

To summarize, in the opening prayer you ask for help, place yourself in a Chi Ball for protection, go to the Temple of Light and invoke the presence and assistance of the angels, archangels and other beings of Light. Furthermore, in the prayer you connect with the spirit and deva of your home, since cooperating with them will allow all the work to be done in an attitude of co-creation. At the end of the prayer you set the intention of what you wish to manifest for the space.

Working With The Spirit And The Deva Of Your Home

The spirit and the deva of the home are neutral beings. They are there to help, but you have to give them instructions. The problem is that since they are neutral it is possible that they may have collected negative instructions or accumulated negative energies from previous residents. But if you give them positive things to do, they will do them. So it is necessary to reprogram the spirit and the deva of the home to remove negative programs they may have absorbed and give them instructions to serve the highest good of all. This is considered a positive reprogramming.

Below is a process to remove any negative programs that may exist in the spirit and deva of your home and to install positive programming. This initial process is a vital component of the energy clearing practice. By doing this process before beginning the energy clearing itself, you will achieve a vital connection with the forces of nature and have the full cooperation of the spirit and the deva of your home. In this way the work is done in an attitude of co-creation with the natural elements and the result is more effective. Since it is a karmic process, you also invoke the presence of the Angels of Karma to assist you.

Karmic Process to Free The Spirit And The Deva Of The Home From Negative Programs And To Install Positive Programs

1. Feel your heart and feel the peace in your heart.
2. With intention, fill yourself with Light. Feel the Light through your body.
3. Put yourself in a Chi ball for protection.
4. Intend to go to the Temple of Light[11]
5. Invoke the presence of Archangel Gabriel.
6. Invoke the presence of Archangel Michael and the angels of protection and purification.
7. Invoke the presence of the Angels of Karma.
8. Intend to bring to the Temple the space you are working with and the spirit and the deva of the space.
9. Ask the spirit and the deva of the space whether they give you permission to do this process. Reassure them that you will do the process with all your love and respect.

---

11   If you are doing other processes on the same day, you do not need to go to the Temple of Light and return for each process. You can simply go to the Temple of Light once when you begin all the process and return from the Temple of Light when you have completed all the processes of the day

10. Ask that all negative energy that may exist in the spirit and the deva of the space be dissolved.
11. Radiate Light for two to three minutes until you feel that the negative energy is dissolved.
12. Communicate the following directly to the spirit and the deva of the space:

With great respect and deep love I request the assistance of the Angels of Karma and all the other beings of Light who are present so the spirit and the deva of this space may be freed from all negative programming and other negative energies that may prevent them from serving the Light.

I ask that the spirit and the deva of the space return to their original mission of Light and that all their work, energies and intentions are completely dedicated to the divine Light.

I make these requests for all time and all space and may this cleansing, liberation and release be effective immediately.

13. Ask the Angels of Karma if the requests have been granted. After asking, close your eyes and feel your heart. If your heart feels expanded and at peace, the requests have been granted. If there is any contraction in your heart, then the petitions have not been granted. If the petitions are granted, continue with the following steps.
14. If the petitions are not granted, you can make them again. If after making the requests several times (you should not make the petitions more than three times), then it is confirmed that the petitions are not granted. It is possible that you may need to wait until you do the complete energy clearing of the space, as detailed

in the following chapters of the book. In this case, you can do the process again after finishing the energy clearing of the space. It is also possible that you may need to make each request individually. However, usually these requests are granted immediately.

15. Radiate the space until you feel that positive programs have been installed in the spirit and the deva of the space; from three to five minutes.

16. Thank Archangel Gabriel, Archangel Michael, the angels of protection and purification and the Angels of Karma.

17. Thank the spirit and the deva of the space for their cooperation.

18. Return from the Temple of Light with gratitude in your heart for the blessings received.

Lost Souls

In some instances negative energy in a space may be caused by lost souls. To determine whether this is the case, it is helpful that as part of the energy clearing process you determine whether there are lost souls present and if so, do a process that will help the lost souls return with the Light.

When a person makes the transition[12] from the physical body, the soul has several opportunities to return to the Light. Unfortunately, these opportunities are limited and if the soul

---

12 Transition refers to the moment when a soul leaves the physical body and returns to the soul dimension.

does not go with the Light at the moment of death, it can remain stuck in the physical planes. There are souls who have been wandering in the physical world for thousands of years.

Some souls do not go with the Light because as they leave the physical body they are overcome by fear and lose the opportunity to make the full transition. At other times, the souls have very strong attachments to loved ones or material belongings and refuse to break away from the ties that bind them to the physical dimension. This often happens when there are strong bonds to a spouse, a family member or a property. Sudden death is another situation where souls may not go with the Light. In this case, the persons die and don't realize that they are dead. They stay in the physical dimension, confused and not knowing what to do. In other cases, souls refuse to go with the Light because they have unresolved issues to take care of.

A lost soul does not belong in the human physical dimension and it is detrimental for them to be here since they are not progressing spiritually while in this dimension. Lost souls are usually harmless.

An important role in our spiritual path is to help lost souls make their full transition and thus ensure their progression. Often, when we clear a space we realize that it contains one or more lost souls. For the energy clearing of the space to be effective, it is necessary to help any lost souls that may be present to go with the Light.

If there are lost souls in your space, the following is an effective technique to help souls to go with the Light. As with all spiritual work, it is important that this process be done with an attitude of compassion and with love in your heart. You are completely protected with the Light so there is nothing to fear.

You can check the space for lost souls by using a pendulum.[13] Simply ask the pendulum: "Are there any lost souls in this space?"

Process To Help Lost Souls

1. Say a short prayer requesting all the help you may need with the work you are about to do.
2. Burn sage or spray *Room Clearing* mist in the room.
3. Place yourself in a Chi Ball for protection.
4. Ask to be taken to the Temple of Light.
5. Ask Archangel Gabriel, Archangel Michael and the angels of protection and purification to help you.
6. Contact the lost soul. It is important to communicate firmly with the soul. You must tell the soul that it has died and is no longer in a physical body. Tell the soul that it does not belong in the physical planes and that while it is here, it is not progressing. Communicate that for its own good, it must return to the Light, to the dimension where it can complete its progression as a soul. If a soul is attached to the house, to people living in the space or to any belongings, tell it that there will be many opportunities of meeting with loved ones and that in the dimensions of Light there are many more beautiful things that will give it great happiness. Firmly state that it cannot stay in the

---

13   Instructions for using a pendulum are included in Chapter 9.

physical plane, that it has to go and that you are going to help it so the Light will come and it can return with the Light. Tell it not to be afraid, that the Light is very beautiful and that God's Love will care for it and protect it.

7. Once the above steps have been taken, say the following *Prayer For Lost Souls*:

Prayer For Lost Souls

Feel the peace, the calmness, the joy in your heart. Relax completely and enjoy the peace that fills your whole being.

Beloved Creator, thank You for all the blessings You give us every moment. Help us so we can do this work that allows the lost souls present in this space to return to the Light.

Beloved Creator, bless the hearts of the lost souls in this space. Bless them with Your Grace and help them so they may direct their hearts to Your Light.

Beloved Creator, bless the hearts of the lost souls in this space so they realize that they do not belong in this physical dimension, that they must fulfill their destiny and return to the Light of Your Love.

Beloved Creator, bless the hearts of the lost souls in this space so they can let go of all the attachments that keep them in this world so they can go freely into Your Light.

Beloved Creator, bless the hearts of the lost souls in this space so there is no fear in their hearts. Help them to realize that the column of Light that You are sending is the Light of Your Divine Love and they should follow it to complete their transition.

Beloved Creator, bless the hearts of the lost souls in this space so they may see Your Light, follow it and return, finally, to You.

8. Once you have finished the prayer, have the intention of filling yourself with Light.

9. Feel how your heart and your whole being are filled with Light.

10. When you are filled with Light, have the intention of radiating this Light to the lost souls. Intend that they feel the Light, follow it and make a complete transition.

11. If after radiating for 3 to 5 minutes the souls have not gone with the Light, continue praying, asking that the Creator help the souls go with the Light. Tell the souls to see the Light, to see how beautiful and radiant it is and to surrender completely to the Light. Ask the souls' guardian angels and other beings of Light to come and accompany the souls.

12. When you have a sense that the lost souls are gone, you may ask Archangel Gabriel whether the souls are gone (Remember you are still in the Temple of Light and will be there throughout the space clearing process.) You will feel an expansion in your heart when the souls have gone with the Light. If your heart feels constricted, it means that they still have not gone with the Light. You can also check with your pendulum

by asking: "Have all the lost souls in this space gone with the Light?"

13. When the souls leave with the Light, thank Archangel Gabriel, Archangel Michael and all the angels and other beings of Light that helped you.

14. Close with the following prayer:

Beloved Creator, thank You for helping these lost souls return to Your Light. Thank You for all Your blessings. Amen.

Scanning And Preliminary Space Clearing With Sage Or *Room Clearing Mist*

Just as you did at the beginning of the diagnostic process, before you rescan each room place your hands in prayer position at your forehead, your thumbs gently touching your third eye chakra located between the eyebrows. Close your eyes and ask that Archangel Michael and the angels of purification and protection help and guide you. Keep in mind the information you obtained during the diagnostic process described in Chapter 5. You will feel the subtle energies of the space with your hands and even with your body. As you feel the energy, you can identify the places where dense, unbalanced or stuck energies are located. Make a mental note of the places where the energy does not feel right. You can also use the questionnaire included in the previous chapter.

The scan is done room by room using one hand while you sage the room or spray it with the *Room Clearing* mist with the other hand. Make sure that the smoke from the sage stick or the mist from *Room Clearing* penetrates every space in the room including the inside area of closets and cupboards, under the beds, behind furniture and in other closed areas. Corners also tend to accumulate dense and unbalanced energy and they require special attention.

As you scan the room while burning sage or spraying with *Room Clearing*, remember the places that feel heavy, dense, lifeless and that may require more intensive energy clearing work. This rescanning and preliminary clearing with the sage or *Room Clearing* mist will soften the denser energies so that the clearing process to follow becomes easier.

Once you have scanned the room, filled it with sage smoke or *Room Clearing* mist and helped send any lost souls with the Light, the space is ready for energy cleansing at very deep levels.

Deep Energy Cleansing

Once the preliminary energy cleansing has been done in which you scan the space to identify areas where unbalanced energy exists while filling the space with sage smoke or *Room Clearing*, you are ready to cleanse the space more deeply. You do this with the help of the Chi Ball, radiating the space, filling the space with Light and cleansing and harmonizing the energy channels of the space, as described in the following sections.

Chi Ball To Clear Unbalanced Energy

1. Stand in the middle of the room and prepare a Chi ball.
2. Intend for the ball to get bigger and bigger, until it is bigger than the room.
3. Visualize the ball expanding beyond the walls, beyond the ceiling and floor, pushing out all the dense energy in the room.
4. Intend that any imprint of unbalanced energy[14] in the walls be completely dissolved.
5. Do the above steps in each room of the house or apartment.

Radiating The Space And Filling It With Light

Whenever you remove dense energy from a space, it is necessary to fill it with Light. Otherwise, the space remains empty and negative energies can easily return to the empty space. So when all the unbalanced energy has been pushed out of the space with the Chi Ball, have the intention of radiating Light to the room and imagine that the room fills

---

14 Negative energy that results from pain, violence or other negativity can create imprints within the walls. It is crucial to dissolve these during space clearing.

up completely with Light. When the room is full of Light it will feel lighter. Do this in each room of the house or apartment. If you are working in a large room, such as a combined living-dining room, divide the room in sections and work each section individually.

Clearing And Aligning The Energy Channels Of The Space

After clearing all the rooms with a Chi Ball and filling each room with Light, stand in the hall or the main area of the home and radiate the whole space with the intention of opening, clearing and harmonizing the root, creative, personality, heart and spiritual chakras of the space. Also intend to fill the space's sushumna and meridians. Visualize all the chakras and other energy channels filling simultaneously with Light and have the intention that each chakra, the sushumna and the meridians achieve a maximum flow of Light, a perfect harmonization and that all the energy channels are clear and Light-filled.

Chi Ball For Protection

Once you have cleared each room of the apartment or house, sent the lost souls with the Light (if it was necessary) and harmonized and filled with Light the energy channels; make another Chi Ball and imagine that your home is inside the Chi Ball. Have the intention that no negative energy can penetrate the house or apartment. When finished, release the Chi Ball. When letting it go, you can affirm:

My home is fully protected and filled with Light.

The Golden Spiral Of Light

Even after all this work, there may still be corners of the space or other areas that feel unbalanced. Although these spaces are filled with Light at the time the energy clearing is done, you may sense that very soon they will become stagnant and the energy in the space will begin to deteriorate. To remedy this situation you can use the Golden Spiral of Light.

After radiating the space until everything is filled with Light, bring the tips of your thumb, index and middle fingers together and, with intention, form a golden spiral of Light. You do this by making a spiral motion vertically from the ceiling to the floor, from top to bottom, with the tail of the spiral pointing down toward the center of the Earth. With its rotation, the spiral will not only maintain the Light in the area for a longer period of time, but the movement will keep the energy flowing. You can make as many spirals as you want. I recommend making a big one at the center of each room, in addition to any others you might create.

Process To Weave A Golden Spiral Of Light

1. Raise your hand with the tips of the thumb, index and middle fingers touching and pointing towards the ceiling.
2. Make spiral movements with the intention that the golden spiral is formed in the place where you want it located.

3. Move your arm toward the floor while making the spiral movements.

4. Close the spiral by pointing the tail of the spiral toward the ground with the intention that the tail is anchored in the center of the Earth.

5. Intend that the spiral rotate continuously and bring Light to the area where it is located.

6. Intend that the golden spiral work forever.

7. Spirals can be made in any size. For example, if a golden spiral of Light is needed for a cabinet, it can be made smaller than a spiral for an entire room.

When you weave the golden spirals, connect with the spirit and the deva of the home and tell them that they can now make spirals to keep the home filled with Light, that they can weave them wherever they believe it to be necessary.

Land

The Earth is a being like us with a soul, a consciousness, and with energy channels that include chakras, meridians and sushumna. The Earth has a heart. It is a generous living being that allows us to live within her. There are many beautiful things we can do for the Earth. If you follow the guidance given in this book, you can make a contribution to the process of restoring our loving relationship with the Earth and to work with and for her to undo all the damage humans have done. We can offer assistance and healing to the Earth and work co-creatively with her so that together we can fulfill our destiny of Light.

Humans have a cruel and violent history of invasions of foreign territories and conquests of native peoples. These acts of violence in which entire races have been wiped out have produced an imprint of pain on Earth. As long as the harmful energies that have remained as a result of all this violence are not cleared, the many sites where these tragedies have occurred will continue to be affected by the resultant negative energies. In these cases the imprint of pain, suffering and violence will remain as an invisible scar. Instead of dissolving, it strengthens and tightens its grip on the energies of the land.

Many of the lands that have become residential or commercial areas may have been at one time sacred grounds used for religious ceremonies or consecrated graveyards. These lands contain the negative imprint of the desecration they have suffered. Sometimes we know where these sacred places were located or where invasions and other acts of conquest occurred. But in most cases we have no way of knowing whether the land where our homes and our workplaces are located has been the ground where acts of violence occurred or if the souls of ancestors are protecting the land or waiting to be released.

As part of the energy clearing process and as a step prior to transforming your home into a sacred space, it is important to work with the land where the house or the apartment building is located. The land is part of your space and it can also become a beacon of radiating Light. The following processes can be done by anyone who wants to transform a property into a sacred space. Releasing the land where your home or workplace is located and freeing the souls of the ancestors who are there, will make it possible for blockages to be removed so that the land can open its energy channels to the Light and be a true beacon of Light for the world.

The Spirit And The Devas Of The Land

When you perform space energy clearing work you can undo negative actions that have caused the land to suffer. An effective way of doing this is with a process to free the spirit and the devas of the land from past negative programming. The following karmic process will do much to allow the spirit and the devas of the land to work with you co-creatively to bring in and anchor the Light.

Karmic Process For Releasing The Spirit And Devas Of The Land From Past Negative Programming

1. Feel your heart, feel the peace in your heart.
2. With intention, fill yourself with Light. Feel the Light throughout your body.
3. Put yourself in a Chi ball for protection.
4. Intend to go to the Temple of Light.
5. Invoke the presence of Archangel Gabriel.
6. Invoke the presence of Archangel Michael and the angels of protection and purification.
7. Invoke the presence of the Angels of Karma.

8. Intend to bring to the Temple of Light all the land where your home is located. Also intend to bring to the Temple the spirit and the devas of the land.

9. Ask the spirit and the devas of the land for permission to do this process. Assure them that it will be done with love and respect.

10. Ask for the dissolution of all negative energy that may exist in the land and in the spirit and devas of the land.

11. Communicate directly with the spirit and the devas of the land, as follows:

With great respect and deep love I ask for the assistance of all the beings of Light who are present to release the spirit and the devas of this land from all negative programming and other negative energies that prevent them from serving the Light.

I request the assistance of all the angels and other beings of Light to cleanse this land of all negative programming.

I ask that the spirit and the devas of the land return to their original mission of Light and that all their work, energies and intentions be completely dedicated to the Light.

May these requests be effective for all time and all space may this cleansing and release occur immediately.

12. Ask the Angels of Karma if the requests have been granted. After asking, close your eyes and feel your heart. If your heart feels expanded and at peace, the requests have been granted. If there is any contraction in your heart, then the petitions have not been granted. If the petitions are granted, continue with the following steps.

13. If the petitions are not granted, you can make them again. If after making the requests several times (you should not make the petitions more than three times), then it is confirmed that the petitions are not granted. It is possible that you may need to wait until you do the complete energy clearing of the space, as detailed in the following chapters of the book. In this case, you can do the process again after finishing the energy clearing of the space. It is also possible that you need to make each request individually. However, usually these requests are granted immediately.

14. Radiate the land until you feel that it is completely free of all negative programming and that positive programs have been installed in the spirit and the devas of the land.

15. Thank Archangel Gabriel, Archangel Michael, the angels of protection and purification and the Angels of Karma.

16. Thank the spirit and the devas of the land for their cooperation.

17. Return from the Temple of Light with gratitude in your heart for the blessings received.

The Souls Of The Ancestors Of The Land

Another serious difficulty found in a land occurs when the souls of the ancestors remain in the land where they have been conquered, killed and buried. Or they may be the souls of ancestors buried in sacred grounds. They may have vowed to protect the land and their presence can bring serious energy imbalance to the land and to those who live on it. The souls of these ancestors need to be liberated from these outdated promises so that their souls may return to the Light.

Karmic Process For Releasing The Souls Of The Ancestors Of The Land And Recovering The Land's Harmony And Light

1. Feel your heart. Feel the peace in your heart.
2. Fill yourself with Light and feel the Light filling you completely.
3. Put yourself in a Chi ball for protection.
4. Have the intention of going to the Temple of Light.
5. Invoke the presence of Archangel Gabriel.
6. Invoke the presence of Archangel Michael and the angels of protection and purification.
7. Invoke the presence of the Angels of Karma.
8. Intend to bring to the Temple of Light the land where your home is located.
9. Invoke the presence of the spirit and the devas of the land.
10. Invite the souls of the ancestors who are still on the property to join you. Ask the souls of the ancestors, the spirit and the devas of the land for permission to

do this process. Reassure them that you will do it with all your love and respect.

11. Direct yourself to the ancestors of the land, as follows:

With great respect and deep love I ask for the assistance of all the beings of light that are present to release the souls of the ancestors who are still on this land of all the commitments made to protect this land in the past, present and future and that prevent them from going with the Light.

I ask for the assistance of all the angels and other beings of Light so that all these commitments are dissolved with the Light.

I make these requests for all time, all space and ask that this release occur immediately.

12. Ask the Angels of Karma if the requests have been granted. After asking, close your eyes and feel your heart. If your heart feels expanded and at peace, the requests have been granted. If there is any contraction in your heart, then the petitions have not been granted. If the petitions are granted, continue with the following steps.

13. If the petitions are not granted, you can make them again. If after making the requests several times (you should not make the petitions more than three times), then it is confirmed that the petitions are not granted. It is possible that you may need to wait until you do the complete energy clearing of the space, as detailed in the following chapters of the book. In this case, you can do the process again after finishing the energy clearing of the space. It is also possible that you need

to make each request individually. However, usually these requests are granted immediately.

14. Make the following invocation:
    I invoke the Light and the Divine Presence
    so that this land may recover the harmony it has lost,
    so that it can be transformed into a beacon of radiant Light.

15. Radiate the land until you feel that it is completely free of all unbalanced energies, filled with Light and all its energies perfectly harmonized.

16. Make the following invocation:
    I invoke the Light and the Divine Presence
    so that the ancestors still residing in this land can go with the Light.

17. Radiate the ancestors until you feel that they have gone with the Light.

18. Thank Archangel Gabriel, Archangel Michael, the angels of protection and purification and the Angels of Karma.

19. Thank the spirit and the devas of the land for their cooperation.

20. Return from the Temple of Light and be thankful for the blessings received.

After finishing these processes, continue with the next step of the space energy clearing process. The process that begins in the next chapter involves identifying and curing any geopathic stress that exists in the space. A description of geopathic stress is offered as well as the process to cure it.

8

Geopathic Stress

The Earth

The Earth is an electromagnetic being like us. Her intricate
energy systems are similar to our lymphatic, circulatory and
nervous systems. These energy grids traverse the globe both
on and beneath the surface and they cover the entire Planet.
These energy lines often crisscross and form intersection points.
The networks have thousands of energy channels, like the
meridians of humans. In all energy work related to the Earth
it is important to identify where these energy lines or channels
are located, where they intersect and understand clearly how
the energy of these lines and intersection points affect all life
on Earth.

Civilizations such as the ancient Egyptians, the Druids
and Vikings have recognized the great power of the Earth's

energy grids. They developed esoteric methods to identify these networks, especially the points where the lines intersect since it is at these points that the forces of nature are most powerful. They used this secret and mystical knowledge –confined to priests, mystics and others who were regarded as spiritually advanced– to build the world's great spiritual monuments such as the pyramids, temples and cathedrals.

These places of intersection of energy lines where spiritual monuments were built were considered divine portals. At these portals the physical dimensions could open out into the spiritual dimensions. Therefore, it was believed that to visit these temples and other sacred places helped visitors to connect to very high spiritual planes. The Gothic cathedrals of Europe, the pyramids in different parts of the world, the prehistoric monoliths of Stonehenge in England, and many other sacred places were built on sites where there were powerful intersections of Earth energy lines.

This grid system of the Earth is an energy system that occurred naturally and had a key role in the health and general welfare of the Earth and her inhabitants. The grid system was there to help us be in more perfect harmony with the spiritual planes. This was a very beautiful gift bequeathed to us by our Creator.

Unfortunately, the situation has changed dramatically since ancient times. This system of energy grids is completely unbalanced today. On account of the deleterious actions of human beings, the Earth is continuously abused and at present the energy grids are in disharmony and greatly affected by negative energies. Physical contamination has poisoned the energy grids and the lethal energies that humans produce constantly as a result of toxic wastes, continuous warfare, massacres, torture and other horrific acts, have created an imprint of pain and violence on the entire planet and contaminated its vital energy lines.

We can only imagine what happens to the subtle energy channels of the Earth every time a bomb explodes; whenever genocide breaks out; as oil, pesticides and other poisons spill into the oceans, into the air. We can only imagine the effects of the toxic waste dumped in the waters and the soil, the garbage strewn everywhere filled with plastics and other petroleum derivatives that never break down. We can only imagine the negative energies that obstruct the vital forces of the Earth every time someone hates, every time someone exploits others, every instant in which a person hurts other living beings on purpose.

So instead of affirming life, serving as divine portals and being life-giving sources for all living beings, the Earth grids are now sick, unbalanced and emit their disharmonized energy to everything and everyone on the planet.

The sacred places that were built on energetic lines of intersection are no longer offering the spiritual benefits they once did. On the contrary, these intersecting lines are now creating difficult situations, not only to Earth but also to all living beings that have contact with them.

The Suffering Earth

The unbalanced energy lines that crisscross the Earth cause what is called geopathic stress. The word "geopathic" derives from the Greek words "geo" and "pathos." "Geo" means earth and "pathos" means disease or suffering. Thus the term "geopathic" means "the Earth's suffering or disease."

Geopathic stress can cause a number of serious conditions such as anxiety, irritability, loss of appetite, insomnia, nightmares, sleepwalking, night terrors, cramps, cancer, muscle aches, chronic fatigue, emotional problems, hyperactivity, aggression, chronic headaches, asthma, hormone imbalances, miscarriages, infertility, imbalance in the energy channels and many other serious conditions. For this reason it is essential to understand what geopathic stress is and learn to neutralize and, preferably, cure it.

To assist in this understanding, the following is a description of the most well-known energy lines and grids that surround the Earth and their effects on the energies of the Earth and the beings who inhabit it.

Ley Lines

In the early twentieth century, the Englishman Alfred Watkins made a stunning discovery. One day while he scrutinized the map of a region of England he experienced what he called a flash of light and in a clairvoyant vision he saw a series of nearly straight energy lines that connected a number of ancient monuments. As a result, Watkins embarked on a line of research in different parts of the world and discovered that the monuments, temples, cathedrals and other places considered sacred, without exception, were located on intersections of energy lines. Watkins named these "ley lines." "Ley" is an Anglo-Saxon word that means meadow. According to Watkins' theory, these powerful lines linked the holy sites energetically. An interesting discovery made by Watkins was that if the ley lines passed through an area of decomposed organic matter such as a cemetery or a polluted river, they became very powerful and their effects were extremely negative.

The Hartmann Grid

This grid was discovered by the German physician Ernst Hartmann during World War II. Dr. Hartmann noted that almost without exception, patients who died of cancer or other serious diseases slept in places where there were harmful energy lines. Dr. Hartmann identified specific houses where people died of cancer and concluded that the position of the lines in relation to the position in which the person slept in the bed determined the type of cancer developed. For example, if the lines passed through the head, the person could develop a brain tumor. If the lines passed through the chest, their energy could cause lung cancer. In addition, both Dr. Hartmann and other European doctors found that gypsies do not suffer from conditions caused by geopathic stress due to their mobility.

The Hartmann Grid contains the Earth's electromagnetic flow. The lines or channels of the grid crisscross the Earth from north to south and from east to west. This grid is similar to the nervous system of the Earth.

The Hartmann Grid has been profoundly and negatively affected by modern communication systems that have placed excessive electromagnetic forces on the energy lines of this grid. Television, radio, cellular telephones and microwave ovens are some of the modern technologies that have harmfully affected the Hartmann Grid. The situation can only worsen as these technologies are used by more people and with increasing frequency.

The excess of negative energy created by modern communication methods has resulted in a devastating situation on Earth. It is as if this grid had been continuously bombed with negative substances until irreversibly damaged.

As in all situations of geopathic stress, imbalance or "disease" is more apparent and stronger in places where two or more lines intersect.

Geopathic Grid

Another network of lines or energy channels that course through the Earth is called the "geopathic grid." The lines of the geopathic grid cut across the earth in different directions and tend to travel through underground water streams or where there are geological formations, mineral deposits or cracks in the Earth.

This grid was the Planet's digestive system that naturally removed toxins from the body of the Earth. The grid worked well for thousands of years, but due to the detrimental actions of humans, it is now emitting harmful energies.

Curry Lines

These lines, discovered by Dr. Manfred Curry, are electrically charged fields that form a global grid. Its lines run diagonally to the poles. Curry Lines are only harmful when they cross an underground water current or are affected by the energies of cell phone stations or towers.

Black Lines

In addition to the grids and lines mentioned above, there are also the so-called "black lines" that are more difficult to define. When a ley line runs through a cemetery or a subterranean water stream that is badly polluted with poisons, pesticides and other harmful chemicals, black energy lines are produced. Black lines retain an extremely harmful force and, unlike the Hartmann grid, geopathic grids and Curry lines, black lines do not have any pattern. They can go in any direction and can form curves, straight lines, exist below ground level or even at ground level.

In short, the Earth's energy networks or grids and their lines are energy transportation systems in the body of the whole globe. If these systems have lost their vital energies and emit flawed energy, they cause disturbances to the Earth and the Earth's inhabitants. In places where there is an intersection of two or more negative energy lines, the damage that can ensue is more serious. A person who sleeps or works at the intersection of two or more of these energy channels may suffer from serious conditions such as immune system problems, depression, cancer, multiple sclerosis and other physical, mental or emotional conditions.

There are countless negative effects produced by the grids and power lines described above, including increased viral diseases, bacteria, insomnia, migraines and many others. There are also adverse effects on plants and animals. A notable example of this is when trees grow crooked or bent because they are trying to avoid an intersection of negative energy lines.

Geopathic Stress And Sleep

Sleeping in an area affected by geopathic stress causes many disturbances since a large part of your body is exposed to the negative energy lines during the night when the energies of geopathic stress are strongest.

During sleep the cells of your body regenerate and much healing occurs during this time. Eighty percent of your new cells are created during this process of regeneration that occurs every night while you sleep. As you sleep, in addition, your brain signals to the physical body the proper level of vitamins and minerals to be absorbed and adjusts the balance of your hormones. Sleep also offers your body and mind the opportunity to rest and recover the energy lost during the day.

Geopathic stress interferes with these vital processes and weakens your immune system. If you sleep in a place with geopathic stress, your body is forced to spend this time that should be dedicated to rest, healing and regeneration struggling instead against the negative energies of geopathic stress. As a result, you wake up tired and listless. We spend more than a third of our lives sleeping, so it is extremely important that the place where we sleep is free from geopathic stress. Otherwise, we will suffer from unnecessary illnesses, shorten our lives and our quality of life deteriorates. Fortunately, the harmful effects of geopathic stress are quickly neutralized and our bodies return to normal as soon as the geopathic stress areas that affected us are cured.

In the following chapters you will learn processes to diagnose and cure any geopatric stress that may be present in your home.

9

How to Identify Geopathic Stress

Diagnosis

Geopathic stress is a serious condition that requires accurate diagnosis and curing with proven energy and spiritual methods. We are fortunate to have available to us a method whereby we work with the devas of the home, the spirits of nature and divine Light to diagnose and cure geopathic stress. The techniques described were received by the author of this book during many journeys to the highest planes of Light.

The energies of geopathic stress are strong. For this reason when doing geopathic stress work it is necessary to take the necessary precautions that will prevent weakening of our own energy. Make sure you are rested and in good health when you work with geopathic stress. If you are tired, have a cold or a headache, or in any way feel unwell or weak, it is best to postpone the work until you feel in optimal physical and emotional conditions. This work can drain your energy. It is advisable that you stop working and rest if during the process you feel tired, feel the onset of a headache or experience any other discomfort. You can resume the work when you are rested and feeling well.

If you suffer from any chronic illness, it is best for another person to do the geopathic stress diagnostic and curing procedures. Also, avoid this work during stormy weather or during the full moon as geopathic stress energies are quite strong on these occasions. If you suspect the existence of geopathic stress in your home or workplace and would prefer that a person with appropriate experience and qualifications do the work, contact *Enlightened Spaces,* a consulting firm that specializes in geopathic stress and general space clearing following the methods described in this book. More information on these services appears in Appendix IV.

The identification of geopathic stress lines is important for the successful energy clearing of a space, especially where intersections of lines occur. If, for example, your bed is on one of these intersections you may experience illnesses that doctors are not likely to identify. The worst risk a person can be exposed to as a result of excessive exposure to geopathic stress is the gradual weakening of the immune system that increases susceptibility to disease. Many therapists believe that geopathic stress causes or exacerbates depression and other psychological problems as well as hypertension, alcoholism and addictions.

In the diagnostic process to identify geopathic stress, the first place you will want to look at is where the beds are located since, as mentioned above, vulnerability to geopathic stress increases during sleep. If geopathic stress is found where the beds are situated, you should relocate the beds as well as cure the lines.

Nature gives us clear indications of areas where geopathic stress occurs. Places where lightning frequently hits tend to be contaminated with geopathic stress. Vultures, snakes, snails and many insects such as ants, moths, beetles, bees and wasps tend to gather in areas of geopathic stress. Parasites, bacteria and viruses are also plentiful in places affected by geopathic stress and for this reason it difficult to treat persons with viral and bacteria-based conditions when they live in places where geopathic stress prevails. Almost all mammals avoid geopathic stress areas. Horses and cows kept in stables affected by geopathic stress often become ill and can be prone to injuries.

The growth of trees can give you an accurate indication of places where there is geopathic stress. Oak trees grow well in areas influenced by geopathic stress. Also redwood, ash and elderberry trees thrive in areas exposed to geopathic stress. However, geopathic stress can impede the growth of shrubs and grass and cause the distorted growth of some trees. Fruit trees are the most likely to be affected by geopathic stress. Fruit trees often do not produce fruit and their trunks are frequently ulcerated in affected places.

Animals and children have good instincts for geopathic stress. If you notice that a child wakes up in the morning on one side or a corner of the bed or crib, he or she may be avoiding sleeping on a line or intersection point of geopathic stress lines. Sometimes children refuse to sleep in their beds because of the discomfort caused by geopathic lines crossing.

If your dog refuses to sleep in a bed, but the cat enjoys sleeping there, you should move the bed. Dogs and most animals tend to avoid places of geopathic stress. However, cats often sleep in places where there is geopathic stress because cats are agents of transmutation and it is their mission on Earth to transmute negative energies into positive energies. To fulfill their mission they sleep in places of geopathic stress. In doing so, they collect the negative energies in their fur. When they collect the maximum amount of negative energy possible, they get up and lick their fur to eliminate the negative energy. So if there is a preferred place where the cat likes to sleep this is usually an indication of geopathic stress that needs to be cured.

The Pendulum As A Diagnostic Tool

The pendulum is a very useful diagnostic tool to detect geopathic stress lines. The use of the pendulum is an ancient art that, guided by our intuition and inner wisdom, gives us answers to questions about subtle energies and other influences that are not detectable by mechanical instruments.

Choosing Your Pendulum

The use of a metal pendulum is recommended when working with geopathic stress as crystal or quartz pendulums are not dense enough and can absorb the negative energy of geopathic stress in large quantities and very quickly. This would require the constant clearing of the pendulum while working.

Choose a metal pendulum that wants to work with you. Just take the pendulum that you are drawn to in your hands and feel if it is a tool with which you can work. Intend to be in your heart feeling the peace and openness in your heart.

Then, ask the pendulum if it wants to work with you in curing geopathic stress. If you feel an expansion in your heart this means that the pendulum wants to work with you. If you feel a contraction in your heart, the pendulum was not meant to do this work and you should do the process with other pendulums until you find one that is willing to work with you in this area.

Once you have chosen your pendulum, clear it of negative energies and the energies of others who have touched it. Just radiate it with the intention of removing all negative energy. When you feel that it is free of negative energy, radiate it with the intention of filling it with Light.

If you feel that the pendulum is heavily laden with negative energy, you can do additional energy clearing by using the following methods. Regardless of the method you use, once the pendulum is clear of negative energy, be sure to radiate it to fill it with Love and Light:

- Pass the pendulum through the smoke of lighted incense or sage with the intention of removing all negative energy.
- Spray it with *Room Clearing* mist.
- Rinse it in water containing sea salt with the intention of removing all negative energy. Rinse it in clear water afterwards to remove all the salt and dry well.
- Place it under a pyramid for 24 hours.
- Place it in the sun for at least three hours.
- Place it under a full moon during the night.

Any instrument used for spiritual work should be dedicated to the Light. This ensures that the tool works effectively for the spiritual purposes for which it is intended. The following is a ceremony you can perform to dedicate your pendulum to the Light. It is always a good idea to also dedicate yourself to the Light so that your whole life will be guided by the highest energies and intentions. You can perform this ceremony outside in nature or in front of an altar of your own making. Later in the book, you will find suggestions on how to create your own altar. The ceremony should be repeated at least once a year, but you can perform it as many times as you wish.

Ceremony To Dedicate Your Pendulum And Yourself To The Light

1. Sit in front of your altar in a meditative state.
2. Have the intention of being at the Temple of Light.
3. Invoke the presence of Archangel Gabriel.
4. Invoke the presence of all the angels, archangels and beings of the highest Light who wish to join you. You will be surrounded by angels, archangels, seraphim and other beings of Light. The protectors of divine Light will also be with you.
5. Have the intention of being in your heart. Feel the peace and Light in your heart.
6. Have the intention of filling yourself with Light.
7. When you are completely in your heart, in a meditative state and filled and surrounded by the Light, say the following from the depths of your heart:

I dedicate my whole self in all of my existences to the Light. (Repeat three times)
I dedicate this pendulum to the Light and only to the Light and ask that a being of the highest Light always guide my pendulum. (Repeat three times)
I dedicate this pendulum to the Truth and ask that it always be truthful and accurate. (Repeat three times)

8. Thank all the beings of Light who are always with you.
9. Return from the Temple of Light.

Using Your Pendulum

The first thing you need to determine is the movement of the pendulum when it answers "yes," "no" and "maybe." These are the only answers given by the pendulum, unless it remains still. If it makes no movement, it means that you should not ask the question that was made or that the being of the highest Light that directs the pendulum cannot or should not answer the question.

To ask questions of the pendulum, follow these steps:

1. Hold the pendulum string or chain with your thumb and forefinger about four inches from the top of the pendulum.
2. Make sure your arm is completely still and relaxed.

3. Make sure your back is straight so that the energy can flow easily through your body.

4. Your feet should be flat on the floor. Do not cross your legs or feet because this disrupts the flow of energy through your body.

5. Breathe deeply and relax completely.

6. Now, identify your pendulum's movements when responding "yes," "no" or "maybe" as follows:

7. Ask the pendulum: "What is a 'yes'"? Wait for the pendulum to swing on its own. It may move backward and forward, from left to right and from right to left or circle to the right or to the left.

8. Ask the pendulum: "What is a 'no'"? Wait for the pendulum to swing on its own. It may move backward and forward, from left to right and right to left or circle to the right or to the left. But the movement will be different from the movement that it made to answer "yes".

9. Now, ask the pendulum: "What is a 'maybe'"? Wait for the pendulum to swing on its own. It may move backward and forward, from left to right and right to left or circle to the right or to the left. But the movement will be different from the movements it used to give the answers "yes" and "no." Sometimes the pendulum string or chain may tremble when the answer is "maybe" or "do not know."

10. Once you know the pendulum's "vocabulary," you can start practicing by asking it simple questions whose answers are "yes." For example, "Is my name (your name)?" "Am I female?" (if you are a woman) or "Am

I male?" (if you are a man) "Are my eyes (color of your eyes)?"

11. After practicing with questions whose answers are "yes," you are ready to ask questions with "no" answers. For example, "My name is (using name other than yours)?" "Am I male?" (If you are female) or "Am I a woman?" (If you are a male). "Am I a cat?"

12. When you are comfortable working with your pendulum, you can start asking it more complex questions.

13. Remember to be in a relaxed state and not to concentrate on the movement of the pendulum. Just relax and let the pendulum swing on its own.

Whenever you use the pendulum, keep in mind the following:

✓ Make sure that a being of the highest Light possible is guiding the pendulum. Before using the pendulum, ask, "Is this pendulum guided by a being of the highest Light?"

✓ Ask whether the pendulum in your hand is energetically clean. "Is this pendulum free of negative energy?" If you use the pendulum a lot, you have to clear it and charge it with Light frequently.

✓ Before asking any question make sure your mind is blank and that you are not emotionally involved in the response.

✓ Do not ask about other people unless you have been given permission. These are most probably questions that you should not be asking.

✓ If you doubt whether or not you should ask something, ask the pendulum first if you can ask that question.

✓ Never use the pendulum while under the influence of alcohol and/or drugs.

✓ When you are asking several questions, make sure that you ask one question at a time. The other questions you want to ask the pendulum are out of your mind when you ask each one. Think of one question at a time and at that moment clear your mind of the other questions.

✓ Only ask simple questions that can be answered with a "yes", "no" or "maybe."

✓ Always thank the being of Light guiding your pendulum and treat him or her with respect and love.

✓ You can use the pendulum to assist you during energy space clearing work, if you have any insight and would like it confirmed. For example, if you feel that there is negative energy in the space, you may ask, "Is there negative energy in this space?" If the answer is "yes," ask if the energy is accumulated in a specific place. For example: "Is the negative energy under the bed?" "Is the negative energy in the closet?"

✓ You can use the pendulum to determine whether there are lost souls in a space and how many there are. After doing the process for lost souls, ask if they have gone with the Light.

✓ You may also ask metaphysical questions. If the being of Light that guides your pendulum cannot answer, you can ask for a being of higher Light to come and guide your pendulum. Metaphysical questions will be answered only if you are ready spiritually for the knowledge you are requesting.

✓ To perform the geopathic stress process, ask that Archangel Michael work your pendulum.

✓ Never let someone else ask your pendulum questions or touch it. You can ask the pendulum: "My friend wants to know ..."

✓ If someone touches your pendulum, clear it immediately.

The Diagnostic Process

In each room of the house or apartment, ask the pendulum if there is geopathic stress present. If the pendulum answers "yes," then you have to determine where the lines of geopathic stress are situated and whether there are intersecting lines.

Start in places where the residents tend to spend the most time. For example: beds, desks, sofas or armchairs in front of the TV. The diagnostic process is as follows and it is performed room by room.

Geopathic Stress Lines

Stand at the entrance of the room and ask the pendulum if there are geopathic stress lines in the room.

• If the pendulum answers "yes," then you have to identify exactly where the lines are located.

• Start by asking if there is geopathic stress in the places where persons tend to stay for long periods of time, such as in the bed, favorite chairs, in front of the TV or desk chairs.

- Ask the pendulum: Are there geopathic stress lines here?
- If the pendulum answers "yes," ask: How many lines are there?
- If it answers that there are more than one, determine if there is a place where those lines cross. This intersection of lines is where there will be the most negative energy that will need to be cured.

Points Of Intersection

To determine the point of intersection, ask the pendulum:

- From which direction does the first line come? The pendulum will move in a certain direction thereby indicating whether the line is straight vertical, straight horizontal or diagonal.
- Then ask: From which direction does the second line come? The pendulum will indicate whether the line is straight vertical, straight horizontal or diagonal. You will then notice the direction in which the two lines run.
- The next step is to ask the pendulum exactly where the two lines meet. Ask the pendulum: Where exactly is the intersection of the two lines?
- Then you are going to go along the line with the pendulum asking: "Is this the intersection?"
- Keep asking until the pendulum indicates "yes."
- Mark this place as it is the point you need to cure in the process described below to treat the points of intersection. You can use a chalk or a pebble to mark the spot.

Your Hands

The hands are efficient detectors of negative energy. Over time and after considerable experience, you may begin to detect geopathic stress lines by feeling the energy in your hands while you scan the room.

To scan a space with your hands, walk through the room with your hands at chest level, palms outward, feeling the energetic changes that occur in the palms of your hands. You may even feel sensations in other parts of your body, such as your scalp or the nape of your neck. As you gain experience using this method, you will feel that the energy of geopathic stress lines is different from other negative energies.

It is possible that as you scan a room for geopathic stress lines, your palms will feel hotter or become sticky or tingle. Each person will have a different set of sensations and this is why it takes considerable experience to identify the sensations that are indicative of geopathic stress when using your hands as detectors.

Your Heart

Your spiritual heart is that place within you that knows the truth and is able to transcend the illusions of your mind to identify what is real and what is not real. Your heart is the best tool to confirm whether or not there is geopathic stress in a place and whether or not there exists an intersection of lines. Your spiritual heart contains all wisdom and with an open heart you can access any information.

To enter into your spiritual heart and access the truth that is there, you can follow the following process:

Process To Ask Questions To Your Heart

1. Have the intention of filling your heart with Light.
2. Once filled with Light, feel how your heart expands.
3. Have the intention of going fully into your heart, enjoying the peace, calmness and joy in your heart.
4. Feel how your heart opens. It feels expansive and very open.
5. When you feel that your heart is open and expanded, you can ask your heart what you want to know. For example: "Heart, are there geopathic stress lines in this room?"
6. If your heart remains open and expanded, this usually means that the space is fine so your heart is not affected. If your heart contracts, squeezes or you feel pressure in your chest, this means that there are geopathic stress lines present.
7. If your heart compresses, be sure not to leave it that way. It is important to bring it back to a state of expansion by feeling the Light filling your heart and opening your heart completely once more.

Observations

When detecting the lines of intersection of geopathic stress, observation is very helpful. By observing the surroundings you can notice plants that are not flourishing, twisted trees and people with serious physical ailments that doctors have failed to identify.

It is helpful to look for places where things do not grow or places in the home where there is clutter. There may be specific places in a home where arguments arise and that is where there is usually a lack of harmony that can be related to geopathic stress.

Notice whether there are problems between neighbors and whether the property attracts lost souls or negative entities. Look at places where garbage accumulates, where there is broken or cracked glass, broken bricks or cracked cement. See if there are mechanical or plumbing problems, electrical faults, vacant areas or abandoned houses nearby. Note if there are places where accidents tend to occur, both inside and outside the home. Food tends to go bad more quickly in places of geopathic stress, so it is helpful to determine whether fruits, vegetables, grains, beer, cheese, jelly and wine go bad too quickly in your home. Even photographic film is damaged faster than normal. See if these situations occur in your home or in your environment.

Imagine that you are a detective and observe everything meticulously to determine the kind of energy you are dealing with. Over time you will be able to diagnose geopathic stress zones in an accurate and efficient manner. Use of a checklist offers an effective method of observation. You can prepare a checklist and as you walk around the property identify possible sites of geopathic stress interference. Include the following questions in your checklist. Many of these questions are similar to those already asked as preparation for the energy clearing. This is due to the fact that geopathic stress creates much negative energy in spaces.

The following questionnaire will help you diagnose areas of geopathic stress:

Questionnaire To Diagnose Geopathic Stress

- ✓ Are there many ants or other insects in a certain location of the property? If so, where?
- ✓ Are there cracks in the walls of the house or building?
- ✓ Are there cracks in the sidewalk in front of the property?
- ✓ Are there disagreements with a neighbor?
- ✓ Are there any vacant or abandoned properties near the house or building?
- ✓ Are there wastelands nearby?
- ✓ Are there places nearby (on the street or vacant areas) where garbage accumulates?
- ✓ Is there a nearby intersection where many car accidents occur?
- ✓ Does the property attract lost souls?
- ✓ Do mechanical or plumbing problems occur frequently?
- ✓ Observe the sleeping patterns of your pets. Where do the dogs or other pets like to sleep? What places do they avoid?

- ✓ If you have a cat, is there a place where it prefers to sleep?
- ✓ Inside the house, apartment or office, where do you feel there is stuck energy?
- ✓ Where does clutter tend to accumulate?
- ✓ In which closets are there things you are trying to avoid, like the things that you never use but keep hiding in a closet because you find it hard to get rid of them?
- ✓ Do some residents of the space have a chronic illness?
- ✓ Does anyone in the space suffer from cancer?
- ✓ Does anyone in the space suffer from depression or constant tiredness?
- ✓ Does anyone in the space suffer from insomnia and/or frequent nightmares?
- ✓ If there are people residing or working in the space with the problems listed above, did these health problems start when they moved or started working in the space?
- ✓ Do the persons' illnesses worsen during the rainy season (when the groundwater flows more quickly)?
- ✓ Do these people feel better when away from the home or workplace?
- ✓ Is there a family member who feels anxious and nervous about the "atmosphere" of the home?
- ✓ Did anyone who previously lived in the house suffer from any serious or long-term illness?
- ✓ Was there a disturbance nearby that might have caused the groundwater to begin to flow in another direction and now it flows under the building or house?

✓ Does this disturbance coincide with the onset of illness or other problems in the space? (Disturbances include: landslides, construction or roadwork, water mains and underground pipe repairs.)

✓ Does the home or any part of it feel too cold or humid?

✓ Where is dead or stagnant energy or a low vital force (not much vitality) found?

These observations may help you detect symptoms of geopathic stress lines and their intersections.

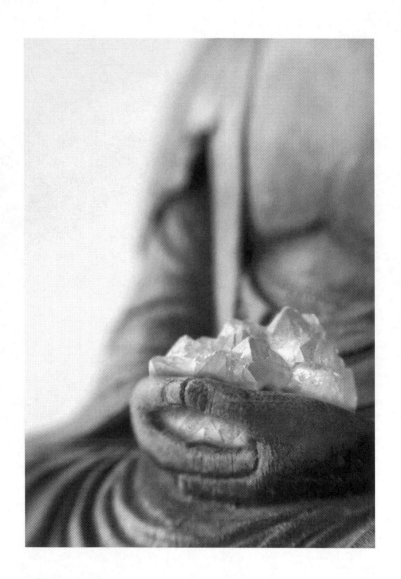

10

Transmuting Geopathic Stress Energy

The process you will learn in this book to cure geopathic stress is based on spiritual energy and is accomplished by working cooperatively with nature. Through this process negative energy is healed and balanced. The main lines of geopathic stress that exist on Earth and which affect your home and other spaces are transmuted into Light. Although there are different lines such as the lines in the Hartmann grid, the geopathic grid, the Curry lines, ley lines and black lines; the process to cure geopathic stress is the same for all.

The experiences of people who have had geopathic stress cured in their homes are diverse and have proven to be successful. Marilyn is a writer who contacted me because she had a serious writer's block that made it almost impossible for her to work. It reached the point where she could not bear to sit at her desk. Moreover, since moving into her new apartment she had started to experience severe back pain. When I asked Marilyn about her work routine, she revealed that when she moved her laptop from her desk to another location of the apartment, her writing flowed easily and her back pain improved.

I performed the diagnostic process throughout her apartment and the strongest geopathic stress lines of intersection were precisely where her desk and chair were, the place where she spent many hours sitting every day. The surface of her desk could hardly be seen due to the accumulation of loose papers, books, pens, mugs and other items that contributed to the clutter. So these were additional indications that Marilyn's workspace was affected by geopathic stress. In addition, there was geopathic stress in the area of her bed and a geopathic stress line crossed right at the point where her back was positioned while she slept. Also, her cat preferred to sleep in that exact spot.

I spoke to Marilyn several weeks after the geopathic stress was cured in her apartment, following the process described in the next chapter of this book. The process included moving her bed to another location in the bedroom. She informed me that her back pain had disappeared and she was so comfortable at her desk that she had progressed greatly with the writing of her new novel. Also, Marilyn reported that her cat had found another place to sleep.

Geopathic stress not only affects homes and workplaces. Recently I worked with a client who lived near a street intersection controlled by traffic lights. A significant number of car accidents occurred at the intersection and serious arguments often arose between the drivers who stopped there. The situation deteriorated so much that the corner attracted methadone addicts who came to beg, harass the drivers and tended to exhibit unpleasant behaviors towards those who did not acquiesce to their demands for money.

I was not surprised that there was a powerful intersection of geopathic stress lines in the street corner. After curing the geopathic stress there, my client informed me that the addicts disappeared as if by magic and that there had been no more accidents. She observed that the drivers' usual impatience and anger had vanished and a more serene and balanced environment had resulted. My client, who had avoided the intersection, now finds the environment so positively changed that she has no difficulty not only driving through the intersection, but also walking by it.

Curing Geopathic Stress

If after doing the diagnostic process you identify geopathic stress in your home or workplace, you can cure it by performing these steps:

1. Transmute the energies of geopathic stress lines
2. Weave Golden Spirals of Light.
3. Place quartzes for the final curing.

As in any spiritual work, we recommend that you embark on the process to cure geopathic stress by being in your heart, feeling love for the Earth, for the space you are working on and for all its residents. Rely on the Light to manifest your intention and feel immense gratitude for the opportunity to do this work of Light.

Step 1: Transmuting the energies of geopathic stress

Process To Transmute The Energies
Of Geopathic Stress Lines

1. Feel your heart and feel the peace in your heart.
2. Fill yourself with Light and feel the Light throughout your whole being.
3. Put yourself in a Chi ball for protection.
4. Intend to go to the Temple of Light.
5. Invoke the presence of Archangel Gabriel.
6. Invoke the presence of Archangel Michael and the angels of protection and purification.
7. Invoke the presence of the Angels of Karma.
8. Intend to bring to the Temple all the Earth grids and the devas of the Earth grids.
9. Intend to bring the property to the Temple.
10. Direct yourself to the devas of the Earth grids as follows:

With great respect and deep love I seek your help and the help and support of all the beings of Light who are present to release this property of all negative energies. I ask Nature, through the devas of the Earth grids, to please release all negative energy present in the Earth grids and that this be done easily and smoothly, allowing it to transmute and become Light.

I have come to do the work of co-creation with Nature so this space can again be whole and fulfill its destiny of Light.

I invoke the most radiant and luminous Light so that all these energies are released and transmuted into Light. May the Light in all Its manifestations completely permeate all the grids and networks, lines and intersections present in this space so that everything becomes Light.

I recognize here and now the Divine and I invoke the Light of the Divine Presence to manifest in these grids, networks, lines and intersections.

I ask that this process be carried out easily and smoothly and that it be for the highest good of everyone and everything on Earth.

11. Radiate the lines and intersections until you feel that everything has been completely filled with Light.

12. Feel the Divine Presence, the radiant divine Love and Light in all of the Earth's grids and in all the geopathic lines and intersections of the space you are working.

13. Thank the devas of the Earth's grids for their help and cooperation.

14. Thank Archangel Gabriel, Archangel Michael, the angels of protection and purification and the Angels of Karma.

15. Return from the Temple of Light.

16. Be grateful for the blessings received.

Step 2: Weaving Golden Spirals Of Light

After completing the process above, do the second step in the geopathic stress curing procedure that consists of weaving Golden Spirals of Light as follows:

Process To Weave Golden Spirals Of Light[15]

1. Weave a golden spiral of Light in each room and other areas diagnosed with geopathic stress lines.
2. Weave a golden spiral of Light in the center of each of the points of intersection of the geopathic stress lines. If you are unsure of the exact location of the center of the intersection, ask the angels and devas who are helping you to place the spiral in the place it needs to be.
3. When you weave the golden spiral, have the intention that the spiral cure the geopathic stress lines and that all negative energies be transmuted into Light.
4. Have the intention that the spirals continue spinning and transmuting negative energy continuously.

---

15   The process to weave Golden Spirals of Light is included in Chapter 7.

Step 3: Placement Of Quartzes

Placement of Quartzes for the Final Curing

The third step in curing geopathic stress areas is the placement of quartzes. This step is very important. The transmutation properties of quartz are powerful and one of the purposes of quartz on Earth is to radiate Light to places of dense and negative energies. This is why quartz is so precious.

Before using quartzes to cure geopathic stress, make sure the quartzes are cleared of negative energy, charged with Light and programmed to cure geopathic stress. You will find a process to clear, charge and program quartzes in Chapter 14.

To cure geopathic stress, a quartz is placed on each spot where you detect geopathic stress lines and especially at the points of intersection of the lines. The most effective quartz for this purpose is clear quartz, which is a potent amplifier of energy. Clear quartz transmutes negative energy into elevated energy. It transmutes darkness into Light.

The process of quartz placement to cure geopathic stress is as follows:

Placement Of Quartz Process

1. Place the quartz in your hand and radiate it with the intention of removing any negative energy it may have accumulated.
2. When you feel that the quartz is free of all negative energy, radiate it with the intention of charging it with Light.
3. While radiating, with your heart full of love, have the intention that the quartz cure all the negative energy in the geopathic stress line. You can say the following in your heart as you radiate:

May this quartz be a perfect instrument of the Light to transmute all negative energy into positive and balanced energy enabling geopathic stress lines to become agents of Light.

4. Place the quartz in the center of the intersection of geopathic stress lines, as indicated by your pendulum.
5. If there are single lines that do not intersect, place the quartz where the line originates (ask the pendulum where this is).
6. If there are many geopathic stress lines coming into the house, you can do this process with a number of

quartzes and bury them in the ground surrounding the property.

7. Use one quartz for each geopatic stress line and one quartz for the center of each intersection of stress lines.
8. You made need several quartzes, depending on the number of lines and intersections.
9. The quartzes must remain in place for at least one hour.
10. Clear the quartzes of any negative energy when you remove them.

If you wish to bring other types of energy to your home you can use quartzes with different characteristics to meet your goals. For example, if you want to bring love into a space, you can use a rose quartz or if you want to bring energies of protection into the space, you can use citrine. Amethyst is ideal for healing. As quartzes have different functions you can combine the healing of the lines and geopathic stress points with other goals you would like to achieve in your home.

When you finish the three steps of the geopathic stress curing process –transmuting the energies of the lines, weaving golden spirals of light and placing quartzes on the lines and intersections– confirm with your pendulum to make sure that all lines and intersections have been cured.

Ask the pendulum:

- "Have all the lines and intersection points in this room been cured?"
- If the pendulum answers "yes", the job is completed.
- If the pendulum responds "no", then you have to find out, with the help of the pendulum, the location of lines and points of intersection that remain to be cured.
- Make sure that all lines and points are cured, otherwise the negative energies generated by geopathic stress will continue to affect the space and its residents.

If you are experienced consulting with your heart, you can ask your heart if your home is free of geopathic stress. With its expansion and openness, your heart will indicate to you that the space is free of geopathic stress lines. If your heart contracts, this indicates that the space is still affected by geopathic stress.

When you receive confirmation that all geopathic stress has been cured, you may remove the quartzes from the geopathic stress lines. When you remove the quartzes, be sure to energetically clear them, radiating them with Light until all negative energy has been removed. You can spray them with *Room Clearing*, pass them through the smoke of incense or sage or wash them in salt water. It is a good idea to place your quartzes in the sun for a few hours to clean them thoroughly[16].

---

16 If you are using amethyst or rose quartz, do not place them in the sun as their colors will fade. Instead, use other clearing methods described in this book.

11

Energy Clearing:
The Final Steps

Sealing The Space With The Golden Spiral Of Light

When the energy clearing of your space is fully completed once you have cured any geopathic stress that may have been present, the clearing is then sealed so that the Light continues to work, heal and cleanse. The space —whether it's a house, apartment, office, land or other property– is sealed by forming a golden spiral of Light in the entire area from the ceiling to the floor. You stand in the middle of the central area of the space and weave a large golden spiral of Light with the intention that it seal the space completely. The process for forming a Golden Spiral of Light is described in Chapter 7.

Protecting The Space With A Chi Ball

Prepare a Chi Ball and place the entire space inside the ball with the intention that it is completely protected from negative energy. Have the additional intention that the Chi Ball protect the space from geopathic stress.

Acknowledgment, Gratitude And Return To The Physical Plane

At the end of the energy clearing process, thank Archangels Gabriel and Michael, the Angels of Karma and the angels of protection and purification. Thank the spirits and the devas of the space and of the land, the devas of the Earth grids and all the other beings of Light who helped you. Thank the Divine Presence for all the blessings received. And have the intention of returning to the Earth plane from the Temple of Light. Return slowly and gently.

Clearing Yourself

After clearing the space, you should perform a brief ritual to cleanse yourself.

- **Cut cords**: Begin your cleansing ritual by cutting cords. It is recommended that you cut any energy cords that may have formed between the space, the geopathic stress lines and your energy. Any connection between you and your space should come from the heart and not from energy cords. Cut cords by making a cutting motion with your hands, palms facing your body. As you make the cutting motion, have the intention that all energy cords that may have been formed and that keep you connected with the space be cut and removed completely.

- **Dry-bathing**: Do dry bathing, with the intention of removing all negative energies from your whole body, as follows:

1. Place your right hand on your left shoulder
2. Run your hand across your chest diagonally, crossing over your stomach. End at your right hip.
3. Shake your right hand as if you were shaking off negative energy
4. Do the same on the other side. Place your left hand on your right shoulder. Run your hand diagonally across your chest, crossing over your stomach. End at your left hip. Shake your left hand as if you were shaking off negative energy.
5. Run your right hand over your left arm from the shoulder all the way down to the palm and fingertips.
6. Shake your right hand as if you were shaking off negative energy.
7. Do the same, moving your left hand over your right arm from the shoulder all the way down to the palm and the fingertips. Shake your left hand as if you were shaking off negative energy.
8. You can do this several times until you feel confident that all the negative energy has been removed.

- **Clearing jewelry**: If you wore jewelry during the space clearing, including the geopathic stress work, remove all your jewelry and radiate it. As you radiate, have the intention of clearing all negative energy. When you feel that all negative energy has dissolved, continue radiating the jewelry with the intention of charging it with Light.

- **Cleaning clothes**: Remove the clothes you wore during the space clearing as soon as possible and wash them.

- **Clearing your aura**: It is also appropriate to pass burning sage around your aura or spray yourself with *Room Clearing* mist with the intention of clearing all negative energies from your aura.

- **Self-healing**: Radiate yourself with healing Light to remove any negative energy from your physical and energy bodies. Do this by placing your hands on your chest and having the intention of radiating Light to your whole self to clear all negative energy and fill yourself with Light.

12

Transforming Your Home Into A Sacred Space

By physically cleaning and energy clearing your space you have prepared it for its transformation into a sacred space dedicated to the Light. Your home now has the necessary energies of Light to radiate not only to the residents and visitors of the space, but it can serve as a beacon radiating Light everywhere. As such, it becomes one more tool through which the Divine Presence brings Love to the world.

The transformation of your home into a sacred space involves several steps that include dedication, sanctification and invocation of the spirit protector of the home. These steps are performed more effectively at an altar prepared for this purpose. By creating an altar in your sacred space, you draw in very high energies to your home. An altar will anchor the Light and provide you with a place to focus on the spiritual planes while finding your center of peace and harmony. Meditating and praying before an altar is most effective because the act of lighting the candles and incense and focusing on the symbolic objects that adorn the altar bring you squarely into the present moment and immediately the Light begins to flow through you.

Creating An Altar

When you create your altar do it with love, tenderness and gratitude for all the grace that has been given to you. If you would like to anchor the elemental energies to your altar, place objects that symbolize each of the elements on a pretty handkerchief or cloth. The following objects are examples of symbols you can use to represent the five elements of Earth, Water, Fire, Air and Spirit. Make sure all objects are free from negative energy before placing them on the altar. Simply radiate them to clear and to charge them with Love and Light.

Earth - sand, quartz, rock
Water - seawater, sea shell, sea salt
Fire - lighted candle
Air - burning incense, feather
Spirit - any object that symbolizes the spiritual realms for you

Once you have created your altar, dedicate it to the Light as follows:

I dedicate my whole self in all my existences to the Light. (Repeat three times).

I dedicate this altar to the Light. (Repeat three times)

Sacred Space Process

Once you dedicate your altar to the Light, you are ready to transform your home into a sacred space. Do the following dedication, sanctification and invocation ritual in front of the altar. Remember to light incense and a candle before you begin. The sacred space process includes the following:

Dedication

Intend that your home is a sacred space, a beacon dedicated to radiating Light continuously. Dedicate your entire house or apartment, including the property that surrounds it, to the Light so that the Light always prevails in the designated space. In addition, you dedicate your existence to the Light.

Sanctification

Sanctification is the act of setting apart something for sacred purposes. In the second part of the ceremony and with an open heart full of Love, you declare that your space is a sacred place blessed and sanctified with the sacred intention of bringing, anchoring and radiating the grace, purity, peace and beauty of the Light at all times.

Invocation

After dedicating and sanctifying the sacred space, you invoke the spirit protector of your home. This protector can be an angel, an archangel or any other being of Light you are drawn to. Think of a being of Light who you feel is close to you and whom you usually invoke when you need guidance or assistance.

In summary, to anchor the Light in your sacred space in an enduring way, it is advisable to perform a ceremony of dedication, sanctification and invocation to dedicate yourself and your space to the Light. This simple ceremony is powerful and will attract a beautiful flow of Light into your space and secure this Light so that it remains there. The ceremony allows you to open the space to receive the Love of the Divine Presence.

Ceremony Of Dedication, Sanctification And Invocation

The ceremony will be more powerful if you perform it in front of the altar you have created. The ceremony should be repeated at least once a year, but you can perform it as many times as you wish to strengthen your commitment to the Light. Remember to light a candle and incense before you begin.

- Sitting in front of the altar, invoke the presence of the beings of the highest Light to join you.
- Invoke the presence of Archangels Gabriel and Michael.
- Invoke the presence of the Angels of Karma, the angels of protection and purification and all the beings of Light who always help you.
- Invoke the presence of the spirit of the home and the deva of the home.

- Invoke the presence of the spirit protector of your home.
- You will be surrounded by angels, archangels, seraphim, other beings of the highest Light, protectors of the Light and the Divine Presence.
- When you are in your heart, in a meditative state and surrounded by the beings of Light, say the following from the depths of your heart, and holding in your heart the space you wish to transform:

I dedicate my whole self in all my existences to the Light. (Repeat three times)

I dedicate this sacred space to the Light and only to the Light and ask that the beings of the highest Light inhabit this space forever. (Repeat three times)

I dedicate this sacred space to the Truth and ask that only the Truth prevail always in this space. (Repeat three times)

I dedicate this sacred space to the Light so that Divine Love and Light radiate from this space to the entire Earth. (Repeat three times)

I declare that this space is a sacred space blessed and sanctified with the sacred intention of bringing, anchoring and radiating the grace, purity, peace and beauty of the Light at all times. (Repeat three times)

I invoke the presence of the spirit protector of this space to care for, protect and help keep this space sanctified, blessed and dedicated to Divine Light and Love. (Repeat three times)

With my heart open and full of Light, I thank all the beings of Light who are with me. I thank the Divine Presence for all blessings received at all times.

Now that your home is a sacred space, it is important to maintain its state of harmonized energy and spiritual purity. In Chapter 14 you will find many techniques to maintain your home in optimal conditions so it may continue being a sacred space radiating Light to its residents and surroundings.

13

Public Spaces

The Earth is a generous being that has given us bountiful gifts of air, food and space to grow and evolve. In nature we are sheltered, nourished and propelled forward by the generosity of divine Love that imbues everything around us. We live in a world where everything and everyone is connected. We are not separate and whatever is good for us is good for our environment. Conversely, what is good for our environment benefits us. Yet, our false belief that we are somehow separate from the natural world has allowed humanity to abuse the Earth and to threaten the very existence of our natural habitats. In order to undo the harm done to the Earth, it is crucial that we awaken to a deep realization that we are one with all that is and that we must honor and respect all life. We need to assume responsibility for the state of our environment just as we are responsible for the conditions of our home.

There are many changes coming to Earth and we can help ease the upcoming shifts so that the new energies can emerge as a luminous rebirth into a new consciousness rather than a plunging into the old ways of the ego that can only continue to seek separation rather than union. For this, we need to work co-creatively with nature to bring a new harmony into the world.

To help us begin to repair the damage done to the world, we can follow the processes we have described in detail in this book and apply them to public spaces such as beaches, lakes, parks, forests, nature reserves and even to large areas such as mountains, oceans and deserts. Buildings that are part of the common weal as are legislatures, courts, cemeteries, town halls and prisons are also examples of public spaces that we can clear energetically and transform into sacred spaces.

Special challenges arise in the energy clearing of public spaces and this chapter will address the processes of energy clearing, curing geopathic stress and transforming public spaces into sacred spaces that can become beacons of Light in the world. To make the process clearer, I will use as an example the process set forth in this book as it was adapted and implemented by a group in Puerto Rico to clear and transform the Northeast Ecological Corridor of the island into a sacred space. Because of its complexity, the energy clearing of public spaces should not be done by one person, but by a group of a minimum of four or five persons, depending on the extension of the area. A good rule of thumb is for the participation of at least four persons for each acre of land.

The Northeast Ecological Corridor

Located in the northeast corner of Puerto Rico, the Corridor covers more than 3,000 acres of forests, wetlands, beaches, coral communities and a bioluminescent lagoon. It is one of the most important nesting grounds in the territory of the United States for the critically endangered Leatherback, the world's largest sea turtle. More than 50 rare, threatened, endangered and native species in the Corridor include the Snowy Plover, the Brown Pelican, the Puerto Rican Boa, the Hawksbill Sea Turtle and the West Indian Manatee. This ecological treasure is now threatened by the rampant development of tourist facilities, lack of water and pollution caused by waste and toxic dumping by military installations.

The Sacred Space Process

Because of the large expanse of land involved, some of the work was done distantly several days before going to the Corridor[17]. With a map of the Corridor and a pendulum César Rivera, who adapted the sacred space process for this area and guided the project, diagnosed the areas of geopathic stress, including the number of geopathic stress lines and where they were located before the space clearing work was done. Four geopathic stress lines were found: two in the lagoon, one in an area of the beach and one in the western coast. This was the only work that was

---

17   Clearing spaces at a distance should only be done by persons with ample experience in the energy clearing of spaces and after completing the advanced workshop, *Creating Your Sacred Space II*, which includes processes for the distance clearing of spaces and other advanced techniques. However, if the public space is small the diagnostic process can be done in person.

done distantly. All the other sacred space processes were done in person.

A group of twelve Paramita Path[18] practitioners gathered early on a Saturday morning at the Seven Seas Beach in Fajardo. From there they walked to the western tip of the Corridor. As they entered into the Corridor, they began to notice that many trees were infested with insects and seemed sick. The wetlands felt sad and tired and there were piles of empty plastic bottles, soda cans and other garbage dumped on the beach.

The group began its work by doing the *Meditation to Enhance Your Intention*. (To facilitate your work, at the end of this chapter you will find an outline of the basic steps in the process). They also prepared themselves for this work with the *Meditation for Protection*, as well as by placing themselves in Chi Balls for protection *Protection*. Once they were spiritually prepared for the work at hand, they did the karmic process to free the devas of the area from negative programs *Protection*. In addition, they did the karmic process to install positive programs and to release the souls of the ancestors of the land, as well as to recover the land's harmony and Light *Protection*. The souls of the ancestors were freed and that alone gave the area a sense of lightness and clarity.

Once these processes were completed, the group did a meditation to prepare them for communication with the devas[19]. They asked the devas if they would work with them

18   The Paramita Path is a comprehensive spiritual path to enlightenment through love, compassion and service to all beings.

19   The Meditation to Communicate with Devas is from my book, *Your Sacred Apothecary* and it is used when working with nature for the preparation of plant essences. The meditation is included in Appendix I of this book for those who would like to do the sacred space process in public places.

and the response from the devas was positive. However, this was a mere formality since many in the group felt, as they walked to the Corridor, that the devas were happy to see them and they were using their Light to open the way for them. Once the devas assented, the group made an offering to the devas expressing their gratitude for the opportunity to work cooperatively with the devas. The offering consisted of three calcite quartzes that had previously been cleared and charged with Light. The calcite pieces were from the property of one of the participants. The participants were not sure where to place the calcite so they asked for guidance. The devas instructed them to form a triangle with the three calcite quartzes and they indicated the placement. When the offering was placed, the devas communicated that they would use the calcite for the highest good of the space to help it heal and to fuse the Light of the Corridor with other sacred spaces created on the island.

Once the offering was made to the devas, the group combined the communication with the space process with the diagnostic process to identify negative energy. The space communicated to them the following: The space was very happy that they were there, but was generally saddened by the lack of respect with which humans treated it. The Corridor complained that people did not ask permission to enter into the space and it asked: "When did they forget that we are One?" The space felt contaminated and expressed that it was bothered by loud noises (from motor boats, airplanes, jet skis). The space also expressed its concern about what would happen to it with the developments that were encroaching upon the area. In general, the group felt that the space was happy and grateful that they were there.

At this point, the group had a snack and then embarked on the energy space clearing processes. First, they did the lost souls process and then they carried out the processes to clear and protect the space. Once they finished, a strong breeze lifted and swept through the area as if assisting in the clearing of the whole area. Golden spirals of Light were woven throughout the Corridor and around the coast. Geopathic stress lines were healed and the group had lunch while quartzes were in place to heal the geopathic stress lines and intersections.

After lunch, participants created an altar and transformed the Corridor into a sacred space. They invoked the presence of the protective spirit and asked it to protect the area. Then they said a prayer of gratitude to the devas, all nature spirits, all the beings of Light and to the Divine Presence for all the help received. As the group returned to Seven Seas Beach, they collected the garbage that was strewn throughout the area as an offering of love and gratitude to the Corridor. The work took approximately four hours to complete.

The group intends to return to other areas in the North, South and West of the island and create a field of resonating Light that will crisscross the island, with the intention that the island become a radiating beacon of Light for the land, all the island residents, for the surrounding waters and the whole Caribbean region.

It is interesting to note that an earth tremor that registered 4.4 on the Richter Scale was felt at 2.50PM in the northeast region of Puerto Rico at the time when the group was performing the sacred space process. This was interpreted as signaling the deep healing received by the Earth and that caused an adjustment in its layers and energy channels. Besides, the group felt that the public space expressed its gratitude by way of this unmistakable message. Many of the participants also felt the gratitude of the sea and fish.

The Sacred Space Process: Basic Steps for Public Spaces

A. Preparation
1. Physical: Bathing or showering with sea salt with the intention of purifying the body.
2. Mental: Quiet the mind, breathe deeply
3. Emotional: Feel the center of your being
4. Spiritual:
   a. Fill yourself with Light
   b. Activate protections
   c. Meditation to Enhance Your Intention
   d. Meditation for Protection

B. Karmic Processes
1. Karmic process to free the spirit and the devas of the land of negative programs and to install positive ones
2. Karmic process to free the souls of the ancestors of the land.

C. Communication
1. Meditation to prepare for communication with the devas[20]
2. Ask the devas: Do you give us permission to work with you?
3. Offering

---

20   The meditation is included in Appendix I of this book.

4. Communication with the public space. Have the intention of communicating with the land. Begin by feeling its energy.
    a. What impression does it give you?
    b. Is it welcoming or rejecting?
    c. How does it feel in general?
    d. Is it serene or anxious?
    e. Is it happy or sad?
    f. Is it light or dense?

5. Ask the public space how it feels and feel in your heart if it feels happy or depressed, sad or satisfied.
6. Ask the land if it has anything to communicate to you. Be silent while you receive a response and have a notebook handy to take notes. Ask the land: "Is there any area that needs more attention?"

D. Diagnosis and Communication
    1. Observation: Make observations while walking through the public space. Connect to the land, to the beings of nature who are there, and open your heart to feel what is happening in the space energetically.
    2. Diagnosis: While you are walking through the public space and observing, you can also perform the two diagnostic processes involved: diagnose areas of negative energies and confirm geopathic stress lines you identified distantly.

E. Physical Cleaning: In public spaces such as beaches and forests, physical cleaning can either be done before you do the energy clearing or it can be done at the end as you return from the area. Remember to bring garbage bags for trash collection.

F. Energy Space Clearing
  1. Process to help lost souls go with the Light.
  2. Prayer and invocation before beginning an energy clearing.
  3. Chi Ball to clear negative energies.
  4. Radiate the space and fill it with Light.
  5. Clear and harmonize the space's energy channels.
  6. Chi Ball for the protection of the space
  7. Golden Spiral of Light to seal the energy clearing.

G. Geopathic Stress
  1. Diagnosis: Identify the stress lines and intersection points with your metal pendulum. In large extensions of land, you can do this distantly or in person with the use of a map[21].
  2. Observation: This is done at the beginning, combined with observation of the space for energy clearing.
  3. Process to transmute the energies of geopathic stress lines
  4. Golden spirals of light. Place spirals in all the lines and in the center of each intersection. Place them with intention that they cure the lines and that they transmute negative energy into Light. If you are not

---

21 Sacred space work can be done distantly but only by persons with ample experience in the energy clearing of spaces and once they have completed the advanced workshop, *Creating Your Sacred Space II* which includes processes for distant energy clearing and other advanced techniques. Please see Appendix III for more information.

sure about the locations of the stress lines, ask the devas who are working with you to place the spirals exactly where they need to be.

5. Placement of quartzes for final curing, for one hour at least.
6. Verify that all lines are cured.
7. Remove quartzes and clear them.
8. Seal the whole area with golden spirals of Light. Weave as many as you feel necessary.
9. Place the whole area in a Chi ball to protect it from the future formation of geopathic stress lines and other negative energies.

H. Transforming the Space into a Sacred Space
1. Prepare a simple altar.
2. Dedication, sanctification and invocation ceremony in front of the altar.
3. Communicate with the protective spirit of the space and ask, with respect and love, that it protect the public sacred space, all that is within it and all who enter it.

I. Maintenance
1. Radiate the area, and any other public spaces you may have worked on, as frequently as you feel necessary. This can be done distantly.

14

Maintenance of Your Sacred Space

You have worked hard, with loving dedication and zeal, to create your sacred space. You physically cleaned your home —organizing your possessions, discarding what you do not use, letting go of what is no longer useful to you. With the smoke of burning sage or the mist of *Room Clearing*, using the golden spirals of light, forming Chi balls, diagnosing and curing geopathic stress and with the assistance of the beings of Light, you brought your space into harmonious balance. Then you consecrated, sanctified and dedicated your space to the Light. After all your devoted work, the challenge you face now is to maintain this space clear, balanced, harmonized and remaining as the sacred space that you created so that it can continue being a beacon of Light for the world.

This maintenance can become a desirable habit, a loving discipline that you practice in your daily life in a conscientious and dedicated manner. In this chapter you will find many techniques that will help you to maintain your sacred space as a beacon radiating the beautiful Light at all times. You will notice that by maintaining your sacred space, a wonderful change will occur in your life and in your relationships with others. You will enjoy peace, serenity and inner calm. Your communication with others will improve. Your environment will feel lighter and more expansive and there will be fewer episodes of illness and other negative occurrences in your environment. Your life will become an eternal flow of Love.

The Five Elements

The elements offer multiple ways of bringing positive energy into your space. By consciously activating the energies of the five elements of nature in your home, these energies will help keep your space clear, harmonized and free of negative energies.

The elements of nature are the essential substance of all things. Health and healing; our physical, emotional and mental welfare; the environment and all the physical manifestations that we take for granted are affected by the elemental powers of Air, Fire, Water, Earth and Spirit. These elements contain energies that are necessary for life and essential to allow us to manifest as spirits in physical form. As you and your space absorb the qualities of natural elements, you will be connecting with your essence and this connection will have a healing and regenerative effect. Your space will enjoy a harmonious balance with the forces of nature. Therefore, it will become easier for your space to attract and radiate Light.

As you create a sacred space you achieve a necessary balance with the forces of nature that allows you to fully co-create with nature in full cooperation with it. Creating a sacred space and maintaining it is another way to work consciously with the elements of nature that can bring you clarity, grounding, serenity and many other blessings to your life.

Air

Air is the element of the mind. Ideas are brought to you by this element. As ideas flow into your mind you recognize them as probable realities. This gives you the opportunity to choose those ideas that serve your goals and your spiritual aspirations. Air is a spiritual energy that initially brings ideas and concepts that allow you to create and manifest. Air is the source of creation. The element of Air is a primary energy that helps both you and your space to open the energy channels to the Light and maintain that Light flowing.

Smoke

Drawing the element of Air to your sacred space is easy. You can burn incense and sage to bring the element of Air to your sacred space. The fragrant smoke helps remove dense and stagnant energies and brings vitality to the energy of the space. When you light incense or sage it is helpful to pass it around your aura to cleanse it as well, especially when you come from outside or after giving a healing to someone.

When you diffuse the smoke of incense or sage throughout your space, make sure the smoke fills the corners, disperses under the beds and other furniture and penetrates deep into closet spaces. These places tend to accumulate dense energy and need to be harmonized more often than open spaces.

Aromatherapy

Aromatherapy refers to the use of essential oils for treatment of physical and emotional health, to enhance beauty and bring wellness. Essential oils are highly concentrated substances that come from plants or flowers.

The use of essential oils is very effective in attracting the element of Air to your home. It harmonizes the energies of a space by balancing the air of the space, but its effectiveness decreases significantly if aromatherapy products made with synthetic compounds are used. It is imperative to use pure essential oils, preferably organic, since you will not attain the same positive results with synthetic products. On the contrary, flooding your space with synthetic oils containing no vibrations will negatively affect the energies of the space.

To invite the element of Air to your space, you can effectively disperse essential oils throughout the space in several ways. You can use scented candles, making sure that the oils used are natural. A more effective way to disperse essential oils in your space is by placing several drops of the oil in a diffuser. A diffuser consists of a glass, ceramic or metal bowl set on a holder that rests over a tea candle. Essential oils are placed in the bowl over the lighted candle. The candle warms the oil and the aroma that flows from the evaporated oil permeates the space.

You can also take a spray bottle filled with water and mix into it a few drops of an essential oil or a combination of essential oils that you find enjoyable. When spraying the area with the oil mixture, the air is energized and you can feel the heavy energies dissipating, giving a lighter feeling to the space.

Different essential oils have distinct benefits and oils are chosen according to the effects you wish to achieve. Below is a list of the most common essential oils that may be used effectively to draw in the element of Air and simultaneously elevate the energies of your space. Essential oils are powerful substances and should be used with caution during pregnancy. If you are pregnant, consult with your health care professional to determine which essential oils are safe to use.

Bergamot

Like all essential oils, bergamot has antiseptic properties that keep your space purified. It is a scent that relaxes and soothes, relieving stress and calming the nerves. It helps dissolve doubt and the sense of guilt. Spiritually, the frequency of this oil helps to open our hearts to the joy of living, it brings light into the shadows of the mind and assists us in securing the help of the angelic realm.

Cedar

Besides clearing the environment of insects, cedar essential oil is a beneficial remedy for anxiety. It is a grounding scent that brings a frequency of stability and solidity to our environment. It assists us in opening our hearts to forgive others and forgive ourselves. It allows us to find the strength and courage to achieve our dreams. Cedar brings hope and optimism to our lives.

Eucalyptus

This fragrance revitalizes our being, banishing fatigue and listlessness. It helps dissolve mental lethargy. Most importantly, eucalyptus has a healing frequency that is anchored in the primary energy of the Earth. It awakens the gift of healing that we all have within us. With great generosity eucalyptus brings us the gift and power of healing to our very being and also to our space. It allows us to see clearly the incredible power we have for healing.

Geranium

This essential oil lifts the spirits, alleviates depression and brings emotional balance. It contains a feminine frequency that connects us with Mother Nature. It is a comforting and soothing oil that helps us open our hearts and do away with painful memories so that we can heal. This essential oil has very powerful energies of transformation and can be used to help transform negativity into positive energy.

Jasmine

A stimulating fragrance, jasmine increases our feeling of emotional wellbeing. It helps us to communicate with the angelic realm and brings angels into our lives. It contains a very high frequency that allows us to transmit our love and light to the universe as long as your intention is powered by an open heart. This essential oil brings to your space the vibration of a calm sanctuary where you become aware of who you truly are.

Lavender

This essential oil has a multitude of uses and can be employed most efficiently to harmonize the energy of any space. In addition to containing antiseptic properties, it is an effective sedative. Lavender has frequencies that nourish the spirit and bring the energies of the spiritual realms to the physical planes. Its compassionate vibration helps dispel sadness, worry and depression. It helps us attain our destiny as kind and compassionate beings.

Lemon

Brings a light energy to the environment and calms nervous conditions. Principally, it clarifies dense situations by elevating them and it helps us to focus better. The fragrance of this essential oil helps us to attain very deep states in our meditations and prayers. It assists us in being more positive and more open to accept Divine Love.

Patchouli

This essential oil brings to us a sense that life is sacred, but it is also a fragrance that stimulates us to take action when we harbor an ideal that we want to realize. This essence assists us in liberating ourselves from self-imposed boundaries. It brings to us an understanding that just as we care for ourselves, we need to care for all that surrounds us because everything is one.

Rosemary

Although frequently used to relieve fatigue and stimulate memory, this essential oil brings a connection between the physical and spiritual realms. Rosemary helps us remember who we really are and what our purpose is in this world. Through its high frequencies, we can understand that we are not alone and that we have the company and help of the beings of the highest Light as well as the Creator and the Creator's Love.

Rose

This angelic essence has such high frequencies that its light dispels any darkness. Rose vibrates to the same frequency of universal love and its fragrance is charged with compassion and generosity. This essential oil brings us the highest vibration of love and awakens in us a love which, when it touches us, also touches all souls.

Sandalwood

This fragrance lifts us beyond the physical world so that we can connect with the Divine Presence. It brings us to a deep meditative state where we can merge with the wisdom of our hearts. It helps to quiet the mind and emotions so that we may hear the messages of the Light. Sandalwood has been given to mankind to help face adversity with equanimity.

If you prefer to use a combination of essential oils that have been blended and prepared with specific goals for your space, Ezencia[22] produces essential oil blends for spiritual purposes. The blends are created with organic essential oils while they are infused with Light in the presence of the universal energies. Each blend is prepared with a clear spiritual intention to help you achieve powerful spiritual transformations.

Fire

The element of Fire focuses on passion and action. When your ideas arise you need the unique power of Fire to transform your visions into reality. When the energies of Fire are activated

---

22   For more information on Ezencia products, please see Appendix II.

in your energy channels, you feel a creative passion flowing through you. Fire is also a protective energy. Spiritually, Fire brings the ecstasy of being into your life. An essential aspect of the element of Fire is that it can awaken your Kundalini, the inner Light that accelerates your spiritual growth.

Candles

One of the easiest and most effective ways to bring the element of Fire to your home is by using candles. In this instance, candles are used specifically to attract the energy of the Fire element to the sacred space.

By the simple act of lighting a candle we are immediately pulled into a state of deep spirituality. Lighted candles help us to focus on our inner being. A lovely daily ritual consists of lighting a candle for a few minutes when we enter our home. When lighting the candle, we can be grateful for the beauty of our home and focus on our inner being where we find peace and harmony.

Before beginning to meditate, do self-healing or embark on any other spiritual practice, you light a candle with the intention of transcending the physical plane and reaching up to the spiritual plane. You can focus your attention on the flame to help you be in the present, focus and let go of all unnecessary thoughts and concerns of the day.

Water

Water represents the emotions and impulses that move us to action. The energy flow of water allows you to remove obstacles from your path. The greater your connection to the element of water, the greater the joy that permeates every aspect of your life, as you enjoy the flow of the moment and let go of emotions that prevent you from being in the present. Water is an important element in your spiritual life because it lets you enjoy a practice to open the heart and develop compassion and unconditional love.

Charged Water

The element of Water helps to harmonize your emotions. You can strengthen this process by placing small bowls filled with charged water throughout your house or apartment. Water can be charged with the Light very easily.

To charge water, place your hands on a bowl filled with water and have the intention of charging the water with Light. Radiate for several minutes until you feel that the water is fully charged. That way you are infusing the water with Light.

Water can also be charged by placing a bowl of water in the sunlight. Solar energy is very healing. The water should be placed in the sun for at least three hours to charge it with solar energy. Water infused with solar energy is beneficial for dark rooms that tend to accumulate dense energy.

Water can also be charged with the energy of the moon. For this purpose, place a bowl of water under a full moon for at least three hours, preferably overnight. Lunar energy is excellent for restful sleep and it lifts and dissolves negative emotions such as anger and sadness.

You can place bowls of water charged with Light throughout the house, perhaps with a flower floating in the water, and this will promote healing at all levels. By placing small bowls of charged water on your personal altar and in different locations in your house or apartment, you attract the beautiful energy of Water that will harmonize the emotions of everyone who lives at home. The element of Water will also help to balance and focus energy in the space.

Water fountains within the home or garden are excellent ways of bringing the element of water to your space and the sound of flowing water brings you the serenity and peace of the Water element.

Earth

Earth is the element of final manifestation. The ideas formed by the energy of Air are brought into the dimension of the concrete by the energy of the Earth. In your spiritual practice, the balanced energy of the Earth offers the necessary and ongoing support that brings you a greater ability to concentrate and to sustain an accelerated spiritual growth. As the Earth's energy is activated, connecting with its energy matrix makes you feel centered, at peace and in touch with reality. This element is connected to your root chakra, the portal of the central energies of the Earth.

Sea Salt

To bring the Earth element firmly into your space, you can use sea salt very effectively. Sea salt purifies and when you place it throughout your house in small bowls or saucers, it collects impurities accumulated in the space. Salt is also used as a protective element in the home.

I recommend to clients with dense energy problems and other negative situations that they place coarse sea salt in small dishes or bowls in the bedroom. In cases of serious negativity, placing a bowl in each corner of the room and one at each window is helpful for protection and also to collect negative energies.

Salt used to absorb negative energies will need to be discarded and replaced with fresh salt at least once a week. If there is a lot of negative or unbalanced energy, it should be replenished every three days. Be sure to discard the salt by pouring it into the toilet. Remember that this salt is fully charged with negative energy and should never be used for other purposes.

Quartz

Rather than being an inert mineral, quartz is a vessel of subtle energies that is aligned to the universal power of life. In the ancient civilization of Atlantis, quartz was used to capture the cosmic energies. By understanding the value of quartz and employing it, Atlanteans were able to communicate telepathically with their ancestors and even with future dimensions. With the help of quartz technology they made tremendous progress in cell regeneration, rapid and complete healing and they succeeded in prolonging physical life. It is said that before the destruction of Atlantis, which occurred as a result of the misuse of their knowledge for egocentric purposes, the wise men of that era programmed quartz with all the knowledge acquired by this civilization so that in the future the programmed quartz would be able to transmit this knowledge to emerging civilizations.

Quartz contains high vibrations that affect all of nature, including our own energetic frequencies. It has powerful healing properties, but more importantly it contains sacred information that if we were able to access it, we could make such astounding progress in our level of consciousness that we would ascend, along with the Earth and all Her inhabitants, to the planes of highest Light.

The information taught to us by quartz is sacred information to be used with great respect, love and with the intention that its use be for the highest good of all living beings. We must remember that the continent of Atlantis was destroyed because of the exploitation of their knowledge for harmful purposes. It is up to us now, the heirs of that civilization, to bring to the world the beautiful gifts imprinted in quartz since the beginning of time.

Quartz and other crystals are strong magnets that attract the element of Earth to a space. Before using quartz pieces, it is important to clear them of negative energies and then charge them with the Light. You can effectively clear and charge quartzes, crystals, gems and jewelry by radiating them with Light. Because of its resonance with high frequencies, quartz charges quickly with the Light. Quartzes that have been cleared and charged become added sources of Light. In addition, quartz can be programmed for specific uses such as, radiating healing Light to a space or to a part of the body. The following is a process to clear, charge and program your quartzes easily.

Process To Clear, Charge And Program Quartzes

1. Enter into a meditative state, feeling the Light in your heart.

2. Feel the Divine Presence bringing you to the present moment as a deep peace fills your heart.

3. Have the intention of going to the Temple of Light.

4. Invoke the presence of Archangel Gabriel. Request his help during this process.

5. **Clearing:** Hold the quartz or other crystal in your hands and radiate for a few minutes with the intention of dissolving all negative energy. For a quick energy clearing, you can spray the quartz with *Room Clearing* with the intention that it be completely free of negative energy. When you feel that all negative energy has been dissolved, radiate with the intention of charging the quartz or crystal with the Light.

6. When you feel that all negative energy is dissolved

7. **Programming**: In this step you radiate the quartz with the intention of programming it for whatever purpose you wish. For example, you can have the intention that the quartz radiate your bedroom and fill it with healing Light, or any other purpose.

8. **Charging**: After programming the quartz, continue radiating it for several minutes with the intention of charging it with Light.

9. When you feel that the quartz is filled with Light, thank Archangel Gabriel for his assistance and return from the Temple of Light.

Once cleared, programmed and charged, quartzes can be placed around the healing table when you radiate healing Light to others. Quartz amplifies the Light that you radiate. You can also position quartzes around you when you are doing self-healing or meditating to amplify the effects of the Light. If you have any health problem place a cleared, charged and programmed quartz on your nightstand with the intention that it radiate you all night in the part of your body that needs healing. The resonating field of healing Light created with quartzes and described below is an excellent way to receive healing while you sleep. By using this method, you bring the element of Earth into your space and, in addition, you set up a defined area to hold a continuous field of radiating Light that will benefit all who are in the field.

Process To Create A Continuously Resonating Field Of Light With Quartzes

To set up the resonating field of Light in a space, follow these steps:

1. Select four quartzes of similar size.
2. Clear, program and charge each quartz using the method described above.
3. When you program the quartz, do so with the intention that the quartz radiates Light throughout the area you designate.

4. Place a quartz in each corner of the room or on the outer corners of the house or building. You can also use the quartzes on the boundaries of a garden, around your bed, around your pet's sleeping area, and so forth.

5. Once you place the quartzes at the appropriate locations, visualize an energy field connecting all the quartzes and creating a continuously resonating energy field that extends upward to the sky and downward to the center of the earth.

6. Radiate the space with the intention that the field of resonant energy created by the quartzes will continue radiating with each molecular vibration.

7. Everyone and everything within the quartz field will receive a continuous healing treatment.

Scanning Quartzes, Crystals And Stones

When you program a quartz, crystal, stone or resin the Light diminishes over time. Therefore, it is extremely important to check the quartz or other stone regularly to determine when the energy has dissipated. This is easily done with the following process.

Process To Scan Your Quartz

1. As soon as you clear, charge and program your quartz scan the energy it is radiating by placing one hand a couple of feet above the quartz and feeling the energy as you lower your hand.

2. Continue lowering the hand until you feel the energy very strongly.

3. Remember the level at which the quartz is radiating the energy the strongest.

4. Every day scan the quartz to determine if it is still radiating.

5. When you scan the quartz and don't feel any energy, you know that the quartz is no longer radiating.

6. If this occurs after several days of having programmed it, you know that the energy only lasts for that time and that every two or three days you have to recharge it.

Types Of Quartzes And Crystals

Quartzes and crystals with specific properties can be used effectively to bring certain energies into your space. For example, rose quartz contains powerful energies of love, tenderness and compassion. Amethyst has healing properties on the physical, mental and emotional levels and jade contains the energy of a protective spirit. Below are some examples of quartzes and other stones that are suitable to invite the element of Earth to your space. Each one of these quartzes and crystals has additional properties that stimulate spiritual development in addition to offering specific vibrations to the space in which they are placed.

Amber

This resin is ideal to help us establish a direct and stable connection with the energies of nature. It serves as a link between humanity and plants, minerals and animals. It helps us be grounded and feel safe in our physical environment. It has exceptional healing properties as it has the power to absorb sick energies, including physical pain. If you place amber on a body part that is sick or in pain, it should be cleaned afterwards to avoid contaminating others with the negative energy that it has collected.

Amber brings warmth, comfort and welfare to a space and neutralizes general negativity. It raises the energies of the space infusing it with a sense of well-being and comfort.

Amethyst

This quartz contains powerful healing properties. It is said that its violet rays penetrate and transform the negative to positive, sickness to health. Amethyst is the stone of spiritual purification and it helps us become aware of our connection with the Divine. It clears the air of impurities and dissolves the shadows so that we can perceive truth. It is ideal to eliminate negative energies from our environment and free spaces of dense and stagnant energies. In addition to connecting us with our spiritual being, this beautiful quartz offers gifts of peace and strength.

By holding an amethyst in your hand during your meditation or prayer, the high vibration of the quartz stills the mind so that you can enjoy a deep and long-lasting connection with the higher planes of Light.

Azeztulite

This wonderful quartz was discovered recently in the mountains of North Carolina to help humanity achieve our next level of spiritual evolution. It is the quartz of enlightenment with frequencies of high vibrations of Light. This new frequency has reached the Earth at this time to help us make a quantum leap in our spiritual evolution and thus accelerate the process of enlightenment. This quartz has one property: The Light and its purpose is to radiate this Light to everything and everyone. Over time, all the quartzes of the Earth will vibrate with the same frequency of Light of Azeztulite to further accelerate our path towards the Light.

About 73 percent of the Earth's crust is composed of quartz. If the entirety of this crust vibrates at the same elevated frequencies as Azeztulite, ours will certainly become a planet of Light and humanity will achieve our potential and become the Beings of Light we already are potentially.

Azeztulite deposits have been discovered now in different parts of the world. Some of the recently discovered Azeztulite contain other minerals, that combined with the properties of Azeztulite, bring even more powerful vibrations to Earth.

By placing Azeztulite pieces throughout your space, your home will enjoy a steady flow of very high vibrational energy. If, in conjunction with the other maintenance techniques described in this book, you use Azeztulite in your space, it will greatly help you to maintain your space as a sacred space.

Celestite

It helps clear the mind and brings clarity to all things. Celestite elevates your thoughts so that you can be aware of who you truly are. It is an angelic stone whose mission is to help the Earth and all its inhabitants to reach our destiny of Light. It offers a balance in the energies and brings calm and harmony to our space. When placed around a healing table, it transmutes pain into a loving Light.

Citrine

This is one of the few quartzes that dissolves negative energy without needing to be energetically cleared. It attracts abundance and many business owners place it in their stores or offices to stimulate and maintain material wealth. Citrine activates the healing energies of the body and clears the mind. But the most important property of this beautiful quartz is the high vibration that connects our minds to the ideal of our soul so that we can express this ideal in our daily lives. Used in a space this quartz can be programmed very effectively to emit vibrations of abundance, mental clarity, healing and to dissolve negative energies.

Clear Quartz

It is said that quartz contains the primary imprint of the Earth, the seeds of spiritual growth and evolution of our planet. Its crystal structure is equal to the structure of DNA that is contained in every living being. It is the physical manifestation of the Light and the Light flows through quartz in perfect agreement, since quartz is aware of its mission as a beacon of Light. Quartz is, then, the Light brought to the physical planes to help us achieve a thorough understanding of Itself. The Creator has given it the task of taking care of the Earth and help her achieve her spiritual purpose. Quartz can be our teacher if we connect with it so that it can confer its wisdom on us. Meditating with a quartz in your hand helps you to align yourself with the Divine Plan.

There are many types of quartz such as rose quartz, amethyst, citrine and others, and each one has specific properties. However, all quartzes, without exception, contain the underlying ability to help us in our spiritual evolution so that we may be able to, in conjunction with the Earth, achieve our destiny of Light.

Clear quartz is extremely versatile as it can be programmed for a variety of objectives. After charging it with Light, just have the intention of programming the quartz for protection, clearing negative energies, healing of specific health problems or anything else you need. After programming the quartz, put it in the place where you want it to radiate Light for the purposes you indicated. For example, if you want the quartz to radiate healing light to your thyroid, after charging and programming it, place the quartz by your bed or under your pillow so that it radiates you all night while you sleep. If you program a quartz to clear negative energy from your bedroom, place it in the center of the room. When using quartzes to radiate a room, it is more effective to use at least four quartzes and place one in each corner. This way you create a field of resonating energy, as explained above, which will have a much more powerful and extensive impact than if you were to use only one quartz.

Hematite

This stone helps us to be grounded especially after a deep meditation when we need to return to the physical planes without experiencing a headache, dizziness or a sense of dislocation. It helps keep us focused on the practical things of life. Hematite assists us in staying connected to the vital energy of the Earth in a solid and precise way. It dissolves negativity in the space and supplies energies that help keep us firmly grounded in the physical plane.

Jade

In Eastern cultures, jade has been used as a good luck charm for millennia. It is the stone of self-knowledge and it helps us to understand the messages that arrive in our dreams. Jade awakens in us hidden knowledge. This stone of protection provides a barrier against diseases and psychic attacks. In a space, jade emits vibrations of equilibrium and balance, combined with creative stimulus.

Quartzes Of Puerto Rico

A few years ago, I was given a beautiful quartz from Gurabo, Puerto Rico. Similar quartzes have been found near the river Tanamá in Utuado. Meditating with these quartzes I find that they have a comparable frequency to the clear quartz as described above. In deep meditation I saw the Taínos, the original inhabitants of the island, pulverizing pieces of this quartz to use the powder in religious rites. I saw clear scenes in which the powder was sprinkled on offerings to the gods to facilitate reaching the spiritual realms. The Taínos also sprinkled the powder on the deceased to facilitate the transit of the soul to the spiritual realms where the gods resided.

I felt clearly an energy of ascension toward spiritualized planes while holding the Gurabo quartz in my hands. I also experienced a simultaneous expansion, an opening of the heart and crown chakras that stimulated the fusion of both. I felt a strong connection with the ancestors of humanity. This quartz brings the frequencies of confidence in life, in oneself and others and a deep peace and tenderness with a high vibration of cooperation and peaceful coexistence.

Rose Quartz

This beautiful quartz of refined vibrations is the stone of love in all its manifestations. It helps us love ourselves, love our partner, our children, family, friends, community, the Earth, the universe and the Divine.

Rose quartz activates the spiritual heart and the heart chakras and helps us open up to universal love. It helps us radiate unconditional love. When one vibrates to the energy of love, one does not think about giving or receiving, as the lover and the beloved become one.

Besides love, this quartz carries energies of compassion and forgiveness. It promotes calmness; heals emotional wounds and helps to overcome anger, jealousy, resentment and fear. It transmutes negativity into harmony. By radiating the energies of love to a space, rose quartz offers a beautiful vibration of tenderness that brings great harmony and a sense of oneness with All-That-Is.

Plants[23]

We share the Earth with animals, plants and the mineral kingdom and we benefit mutually when we consciously strive to live in harmony with all living beings on the planet. Having a pet at home brings the unconditional love of animals into our space. As mentioned in the previous section, quartzes and other stones help to harmonize the energies of a space and bring healing, among many other benefits. Plants constitute another aspect of nature that is important in attracting and maintaining the element of Earth in a space. Plants are conscious living beings and they contribute greatly to bringing in balance and positive energy to a space.

Different plants have diverse characteristics that can be very helpful to us in transforming and maintaining our space as a beacon of light, besides providing remedies for health conditions. In Puerto Rico we are fortunate to have a wealth of medicinal plants that bring untold spiritual benefits as well.

Below is a list of common medicinal plants[24]. The information included was received during meditative states in communication with the deva of each plant. Offering a home to some of these plants in your sacred space will draw to your home not only the energies of the Earth element, but also untold healing energies. In the descriptions included, I do not mention the medicinal properties of the plants because the focus of this book is to help you create and maintain a sacred space for spiritual purposes. Therefore, we have described only the energetic and spiritual benefits of these plants on your

---

23   More information on the spiritual aspects of plants is included in my book *Your Sacred Apothecary*, published by Paramita Press.

24   A more extensive list of the spiritual uses of medicinal plants is included in *Your Sacred Apothecary*.

environment. The medicinal properties of these plants are well-recognized and information about them can be easily obtained from traditional healers and local publications.

Anamú (garlic weed)

Used by traditional healers in the Caribbean as a treatment for cancer and many other physical conditions, this plant contains the frequencies of a very powerful protective spirit. It stimulates the energy channels and neutralizes the negative energy in our environment. It calms excessive mental and emotional stimulation and comforts us with a blanket of serenity. It positions us in the here and now, removing past grievances from our lives and helping us be in the moment. Anamú brings a quiet strength to our space.

Basil

This aromatic plant provides energies of serenity and tranquility. Its fragrance helps to relieve stress and find our center so we can enjoy inner peace. Basil assists us in removing restraints and clearing mental confusion. It protects us from negative energies while inspiring our confidence in difficult moments of our lives. Basil brings harmonizing energies into the space.

Fern

The fern has survived since prehistoric times. It predates the dinosaurs. Ferns became very popular indoor plants during the Victorian era and they have since become a staple in ornamental gardens and interior spaces. However, the medicinal and spiritual legacy that this plant gives to humanity is almost completely unknown.

In dreams I have been shown the many uses of this plant to relieve physical conditions. I have also received guidance on the use of ferns to bring harmony, peace and serenity to the environment. Ferns provide a spiritualized energy that brings peace and opening to the heart.

With its long fronds, this plant offers a connection to the spiritual realms and as such, brings beautiful energies of divine love to a space.

Mugwort

This shrub, also known as altamisa, has the compassionate properties necessary to calm emotional pain. Its essential energy helps to heal the layers of pain that have accumulated throughout our past and present lives and it acts as a neutralizing energy that heals the scars of the heart. With its frequencies of tenderness and compassion, it helps us open our hearts even when we feel vulnerable. It has an energy that nourishes our spirit with serenity and peace.

Physic Nut

This shrub provides us with an energy of relief from emotional and spiritual pain and helps to dispel the cellular memory of traumas embedded in our bodies at very deep levels. I see this plant as a huge eraser that hits the "delete" button of our grief and vanishes the imprints of pain that remain deep inside our being. With very tender, compassionate energy, Physic Nut straightens our twisted path so we can escape pain and breathe in the fresh air of the joy of living.

Plantago or Plantain

In addition to its many medicinal uses, plantago (known as llantén in Spanish) gives us spiritual gifts as well. Its spears bring clarity and focused energies to our spiritual selves and help us to perceive the truth, not with the mind, but with our inner vision. It contains a powerful energy of strength. Plantago assists us in opening to our inner wisdom. It saturates spaces with its clear energies and dispels all mental and emotional darkness.

Rue

The medicinal properties of rue have been valued by traditional healers in Puerto Rico for centuries. The essential energy of this aromatic plant balances the energy channels and stimulates the opening and expansion of the chakras. Its qualities of unconditional compassion offer comfort in difficult times and bring energies of serenity to a space.

Wild Balsam

This vine, called cundeamor in Spanish, relieves our anxiety and stress. It produces a spiritual soothing energy that helps us to experience deep states of meditation. It opens and expands our luminous body so we can connect more easily to the planes of Light. It reminds us that at all times we are a part of the One. It assists us in the dissolution of doubts and fears and brings a calming effect to our space.

Yerba Buena

The calming energies of this mint dissolve any stress and anxiety brought into a space. It opens and expands the throat chakra and is of great benefit for effective communication in all areas. It brings to our spaces a collaborative and creative energy that helps us work with others effectively and without competition.

Communication With Plants

Effective communication between humans and plants is possible and desirable. As has been proven scientifically, plants perceive our intentions. They respond positively to feelings of love, tenderness and care. In the same way, they may weaken, fall ill or even die as a result of abandonment, being ignored and lack of affection, lack of love. Talking to plants is not a sign of madness, as some believe, but a sign that you value the wonderful contributions that nature makes to humanity. Once you have selected the plants that will help you maintain the element of Earth in your sacred space, talk lovingly to your plants and don't be surprised when they return your kindness with beautiful offshoots and blossoms. When you are about to prune a plant or cut its flowers, be sure to ask its permission and let it know what you are about to do. Plants can suffer from shock as was proven by Cleve Backster, a well-known expert on lie detector technology.

One afternoon Backster was in his office in New York City. His secretary had brought him a long-leafed plant called dracaena to brighten up his drab workspace. As Backster observed the plant, he wondered if it would react to certain actions. There was a lie detector on his desk and he decided to conduct an experiment whereby he attached the wires of the galvanometer (a part of the lie detector) to the plant. Then he would burn one of its leaves to observe whether the plant reacted to this action. The lie detector is a very sensitive instrument that can detect slight energetic shifts, so Backster considered this to be an ideal way to determine whether there would be any change in the energy of the plant as the leaf was burned. To Backster's surprise even before striking the match and by simply having the intention of burning the leaf, the galvanometer was activated by the plant's intense vibrations. The instrument's needles began to swing so wildly that Backster realized immediately that the plant reacted strongly not to the act itself, but to the thought he had prior to acting. This experiment has been duplicated by scientists many times using different instruments and in a variety of conditions. The results have confirmed that plants have consciousness and a "knowingness" that allows them to detect the intentions of humans, animals and other plants.

Spirit

The element of Spirit unites all the other elements. It is the sacred element that is present in all things. It is what allows the other elements to manifest. When you are aligned with this element, everything is balanced within and around you. You become one with all existence and you discover that there is room for everything in your life; that there is a purpose for whatever arises. In your spiritual practice, the element of Spirit helps you to access the wisdom of your inner heart. You are able to focus on what's truly important and to know your true purpose.

Attracting and maintaining the element of Spirit in a space requires an attitude of respect and reverence toward the space. The following simple spiritual practices bring more Light to a space and maintain the element of Spirit firmly anchored there:

- Prayer
- Meditation
- Cultivating silence during an hour or more each day
- Radiating the space with Light
- Removing your shoes before entering the space

In addition to the above, there are other practices that will help you bring and maintain the element of Spirit into your home. I will mention three practices that are very effective in magnetizing your home to sacred energies. These are sound, numerology and colors.

Sound

In his research, Dr. Masau Emoto[25] found that loud and discordant sounds such as rock music cause an energetic imbalance that is so great that water molecules sustain structural mutilations. However, when the damaged water molecules are exposed to harmonious sounds such as classical and folk music, the structural damage is repaired. Just as inharmonious sounds can damage water molecules, dissonant sounds such as heavy metal music can cause serious imbalance within a space. Yet, harmonious sounds such as New Age or classical music bring balance to a space and align it with the spiritual planes.

For this reason in almost every religious and spiritual tradition bells and other instruments of radiant sounds are used not only to balance the energies, but also to induce a serene atmosphere of spirituality into the space.

---

25 For further information, please see *The Hidden Messages of Water* by Dr. Masau Emoto.

Bells And Singing Bowls

Ringing bells is a spiritual practice that balances the energies of a space. Before meditation, self-healing or even as you enter your home, ringing a bell or a Tibetan singing bowl will clear, elevate and spiritualize the energies of the space. If you feel the energies of your space are dense or unbalanced maybe as a result of a discussion in the space or because someone with negative energy was there, by ringing a bell or a Tibetan singing bowl the energies will immediately regain normal balance and harmony.

To derive the utmost benefit, it is important to use bells and singing bowls with a melodious sound. Bells and singing bowls with an uplifting sound will also have a beneficial effect on the residents of the space. They calm and soothe emotions and quiet the mind. Silver bells have a purity of sound that is beautiful and restful. Brass bells are often used to promote a spiritual atmosphere in churches and temples. Tibetan Buddhists often use a combination of elements in their bowls and bells to refine the effectiveness of instruments in clearing spaces of dense energies.

Bells, singing bowls and other instruments used for spiritual practices should be kept in a special place just like all objects used for space clearing and other spiritual practices. If you take the bells or singing bowls outside, protect them from negative energy. You can do this easily by wrapping them in cotton or silk fabric that is used only for this purpose. Do not use synthetic material.

The calming notes of wind chimes are also effective in bringing harmonious and balancing sounds to the home and attracting the element of Spirit into a space.

Mantras

Chanting mantras is another way to harmonize energies while bringing the element of Spirit into the space. A chanting practice not only attracts the element of Spirit, but chanting also has the effect of harmonizing any energy imbalance in the home and brings a sense of serenity to the heart of the person chanting.

Mantra is a Sanskrit word that means "divine speech." It refers to a creative and healing universal vibration that affects the material world and transcends it. We could say that a mantra is the vibration of the Divine sound. Mantras are energy-based sounds whose power derives from the vibrating effect that the sound produces. By repeating the mantra, you create a physical vibration that affects your physical body and your subtle bodies and the physical and subtle vibrations in your environment.

On the physical level the nerves, cells and molecules in your body are affected by the vibrations of sound. Not surprisingly, when people are exposed to loud and dissonant sounds, their nervous system suffers. The other side of this equation is that Divine sounds –vibrations intended to heal, soothe and harmonize– will have a positive effect on your nervous system and generate a sense of peace and prosperity. Mantras empower your universal and vital energy, the vital life energy that encompasses everything.

Mantras acquire more power when combined with intention. This causes the effects of Divine sound to amplify and gives you greatly enhanced results. With your intention and attention you enhance, strengthen and give more power to the energetic effects of the mantra.

There are mantras to help heal, protect yourself and your possessions, to heal your karma and improve relationships. Mantras can also help you to achieve higher levels of consciousness and can function as a spiritual "telegraphic" system through which you can invoke divine forces.

Some mantras you could chant, either out loud or silently, are the following:

The divine Light glows within me.

Om (sacred syllable, primordial sound)

Om mane padme hum (the jewel of the lotus –divinity within the heart)

Ha Shem (blessed be The Name)

Elohim (all that is, is God)

Drums

Some cultures use drums for spiritual practices, but I do not recommend their use in a sacred space because I have observed that although the sound of a drum can dispel negative energies, it can also attract them.

Additional Aspects To Consider When Maintaining Your Sacred Space

Numerology

Numbers have specific energies and these energies can assist in your spiritual evolution. Numerology explores the qualities and inner meanings of numbers. Knowledge of these inner meanings will offer your space an energetic boost as it will allow you to consciously select and use numbers whose energies are consistent with your spiritual goals. Consider the numbers in the address of a home, office or apartment when choosing a space. If you are planning on buying or renting a house, apartment or office you can add the numbers in the address to determine if the number vibrates in harmony with your energy or the energy of what you would like to manifest in your life.

The following is a list of numbers with their energy meaning. To calculate a number, you add the numbers until you reach the smallest number under 9, unless the numbers add up to 10, 11, 12, 22, 33 or 40 which are master numbers, as indicted in the list below. For example, if you live in house number 959, the total would be 5 as follows: 9 + 5 + 9 = 5. If your house number is 354, calculate as follows: 3 + 5 + 4 = 12. In this case, you do not reduce the number further since number 12 is a master number. Master numbers represent frequencies of very high energy. These frequencies are potent and possess more potential for spiritual manifestation than single numbers.

Numbers and Their Meaning
Single Numbers

1 - New beginnings, union with God, union with All-That-Is

2 - Balance of masculine and feminine energies. Balance of the physical and spiritual aspects of your life.

3 - Perfect harmony of mind, body and spirit. It represents the divine trinity.

4 - Growth in perfect balance.

5 - A change is happening now or will happen very soon.

6 - Guide, orientation of spiritual masters. It also symbolizes the perfect balance of a human being.

7 - Mystical number representing the cycles of beginnings and endings

8 - Cosmic consciousness, the infinite

9 – A cycle is completed. Completion of the old.

Master Numbers

10 - A new beginning with renewed understanding. A higher frequency of spiritual understanding.

11 - The power to creatively express the divine balance of one's being. A master number that expresses the perfect union with God and with All-That-Is.

12 - Powerful unity of energy. Cycle of growth and development.

22 - Spiritual expression of balance and integration of one's being.

33 - Spiritual master. Spiritual teachings of a high level.

40 - Mystic energy.

0 - Wholeness, perfection.

When you have the opportunity to choose a new space for your home, shop or office, use numerology to determine if the space has good energy or energies that you would like to attract to your life. For example, if you consider a house with the number 920, calculate that 9 +2 +0 is equal to 11. According to the meanings of the numbers outlined above, 11 is a master number that brings energies of perfect union with God and All-That-Is. It brings divine balance to one's being. It is a highly positive number if you wish spiritual progress.

When you move into a new space, you can choose an appropriate number. But what happens if you already bought or rented the house, apartment or office and discover that the number of the space is not compatible with what you want to achieve, with the energies that you want to bring to your life? What can you do?

In this case, it is very easy to draw to your home or workplace the resonance that you want. Simply place a number inside the space that, when added to the numbers of the address, give you the number that you wish to have. For example, let's say that your house is number 832. When you do the calculations (8 +3 +2 = 13, 1 +3 = 4), you realize that the resulting number is 4. As discussed earlier, this number represents growth in perfect balance. However, you prefer the energies of quick changes in your life because you just got divorced and would like to start a new business. So you would want to bring to your space the energy of number 5. To accomplish this, simply place inside the space the number 28 that, when added to the house number which is 832, will result in the following calculation: 8 +3 +2 +2 +8 = 23, 2 +3 = 5. Number 5 will draw to your space the energy of a change that will arrive soon.

If there are letters as well as numbers in your address, you can convert the letters into numbers according to the following chart:

1	2	3	4	5	6	7	8	9
A	B	C	D	E	F	G	H	I
J	K	L	M	N	O	P	Q	R
S	T	U	V	W	X	Y	Z	

Colors

According to research studies in psychology, colors affect our mental and emotional states. The light reflected in all objects around us has an energy that, depending on its energetic density, affects us in different ways. For this reason we must exercise caution in choosing the colors in our space. So that your sacred space remains a place of serene and harmonious energies, it is important that you choose colors that emit this energy in the walls, fabrics, furniture and other elements of the space.

The following are the features of the most common colors and how they affect your space at mental, emotional and spiritual levels. The colors range from the densest in the color spectrum to the more spiritualized.

Red

This is a stimulating color that brings energies of power, vigor, drive, sexuality and passion. Red is strongly associated with the instincts of survival and self-preservation. The color red stimulates us to take action in an energetic and dynamic manner. Red contains an exciting and sensual physical energy. Because of its stimulating nature, it is recommended that you use this color with caution when creating your sacred space.

Orange

This is the color of joy, creativity and enthusiasm. It fosters a sense of emotional well-being by stimulating optimism and self-confidence. Its vivacious energy animates the expression of emotions. As it is a color that promotes socialization, it is a good color to use in places where you want people to gather.

Yellow

Yellow activates creative and intellectual energies. It makes us feel happy and optimistic. It encourages us to be friendly, honest and disciplined. It helps us focus and brings clarity to our thoughts. If we are going through some change in our lives, this color supports our flexibility and ease of change. It helps us adjust and adapt to any alteration of our routine. Yellow is said to bring good luck.

Green

Green is the color of healing, abundance, prosperity and good fortune. It stimulates feelings of peace, balance and harmony. It helps us to feel love, tenderness and compassion. This color connects us to nature. It is the color of purification and renewal.

Blue

The colors mentioned above are considered warm colors. Blue marks the beginning of the cooler colors within the color spectrum. It is the color of balance and peace. It promotes self-confidence and trust in others. Blue compels us to reach the inner truth and to manifest our ideals. With its harmonized and calm energies it helps us to reach deeper states of meditation.

Indigo

This color is a blend of blue and violet. It reflects dignity, knowledge and intuition. It brings mental clarity, insight, balance and wisdom.

Violet

This color is a combination of red and blue. It is the color of spirituality, of the fulfillment of our spiritual goals. Its energies of unity help us to align with the Union of everything in existence. Violet foments a feeling of Oneness with the Creator and with everything and everyone. It is a comforting, soothing and consoling color in times of stress. It encourages us to trust in the future. Its power can be overwhelming, therefore, it is not recommended that you use it to paint an entire room. You can paint an area of a white room or it can be diluted to create a more subdued color like lilac or lavender.

White

This color is the sum of all colors in the spectrum. It is the color of purity, innocence and truth. White promotes humility and understanding of our divine nature. The energies of white, which are the lightest vibrations in the color spectrum, guide us towards a better spiritual understanding and direct us to Divine Love. It contains within itself the power of transformation towards purity and the perfection of being.

Textures

In addition to selecting appropriate colors for your sacred space, it is important to choose natural fabrics such as cotton and linen for cushions, upholstery, blankets and other objects in your sacred space. Synthetic materials lack live energy and, in many cases and depending on the material, may contain negative or dead energies.

It is also important that your sacred space remain free of things you do not like or objects that contain negative energies, even if these things have been given to you as gifts or they are objects you inherited. Make sure everything in your sacred space is vibrating with high frequencies and emitting a sense of well-being and harmony.

The persons residing in the home should respect the space, love and nurture it, care for it and give the space what it needs. If love, respect and nurturing are not there, the space will react according to the situation. The harmony between spaces and their residents can be easily achieved once you acknowledge the needs of the space and provide it with the love, respect and nurturing that it thrives on.

15

The Gift of Grace

Creating a sacred space is a divine impulse that motivates us to find the juncture between our physical being and our spiritual reality. The sacred space you create, with unconditional love and generosity of spirit, is a gift of Grace that when offered to the world opens your being to receive the Grace of our Beloved Source. The more you give, the more divine gifts you receive. You start with your sacred space, a beacon of Light created by you to radiate your environment, and as you breathe in the spiritualized air of your sacred space, you awaken to the deep understanding that you can create a planet that is a cathedral of Light dedicated to the Light. You have within you a great Love, a great Light, and together with other human beings, you can achieve the prevalence of Light in the world.

The world may seem at times like a derailed train headed for destruction. While it is true that a destructive impulse exists in some people, a spark of Divine Love exists in all, even in those who are not aware of it. And their souls, like ours, yearn for peace, yearn for the sweet return to the Realm of Light. But in their state of spiritual evolution, they have not yet been able to peel, one by one, the layers of ego that cloud and hide their beautiful Light. We pray that when they have learned the lessons they came to this planet to learn, their ego weakens, the veils of illusion fall and they will be able to radiate the beautiful Light that they truly are.

And you can help. You begin with the sacred space process, creating a beautiful instrument that radiates Light all around itself. And as you fulfill this task, your heart fills with love until it overflows in luminous waves of Light toward all humanity. With the strength of your love, your commitment to truth, your unconditional compassion you can bring the frequencies of a new consciousness, a heightened and spiritualized awareness, to the rest of humanity including those who, through egos controlled by fear, attempt to destroy the world.

Nothing on this planet, which is the manifestation of divine Love, is evil. Within the Divine Light there is only goodness, beauty, peace. But when human beings allow ourselves to be dominated by our egos, we separate from the Light and create, within our own illusions, an arena of conflict and destruction. Yet in an instant, you and I and all who have seen that there is something radiant and beautiful beyond the illusory veil of ego, can empower ourselves with the Light that we are and that we have always been. We can then deny the darkness, deny the violence and in perfect union with the Divine Presence we can help to heal the Earth.

You have already begun this process of deep healing by creating your sacred space. You are maintaining a respectful attitude towards everything in existence and an abiding faith that you are a beautiful being of Light. You are aware that with your Light you can transform the world, bringing it from an unreal world based on the delusions of the ego to a world of absolute clarity that is one with the Light and everything in existence.

Love is everything and in this Love we are One, rejoicing in the sweet embrace of our Beloved Source.

And what is Grace? What is this gift of Grace that the Creator has given you? The Creator's Grace is the radiant Light of Divine Love that is within you. This Grace, this Light has the power to transform your life by bringing to your understanding the profound realization that you are already one with the Divine Presence, that you have always been one with God. The gift of Grace can dismantle the veils of illusion so that you can be aware of this reality with your inner vision. The Gift of Grace awakens you to the Truth of all existence, a vibratory heightening that allows you to experience at all times your perfect union with the Beloved.

The gift of Grace lets you expand your consciousness to unimaginable heights where you heal at all levels and the bars of the prison of your ego vanish forever. The gift of Grace is absolute freedom to live your life as the being of Light that you are with a perfect unified consciousness.

As you create and maintain your sacred space—even bringing this work to public spaces such as parks, lakes, reservoirs, forests— the gift of Grace will begin to work in miraculous ways in your Life. Your beautiful heart, so full of

Light, opens infinitely to gather within its unlimited Love the heartbeat of existence. The Divine Presence is in your heart and you reside in the Divine Heart. **You** are a sacred space. That is your reality.

May your sacred space bring you the gift of Grace and all the blessings that the Divine Presence has given you already and you only need to recognize.

Love is Everything. And you are that Love

Appendix I

Communicating With The Devas For Co-Creation[26]

Continuous communication with the devas is essential in the cocreative process with nature. We approach devas with love, respect and a deep wish to bring Light into the world. Before attempting to enter the devic world, it is recommended that you do the following meditation that will help you to align and harmonize your energies and to be in your heart, feeling peace and joy.

Beore going to the land or public space (forest, beach, mountain, etc.) where you will work with the devas, do the following meditation that will help you to feel divine Love in your heart and to love unconditionally everything and everyone in existence. This meditation will open and expand your heart so that your work with the nature spirits is based on Love, Light and a state of union with the natural world and all of existence.

---

26   From the book *Your Sacred Apothecary*.

Meditation To Prepare For
Communication With The Devas

Begin by taking a deep breath and as you breathe out, feel your body relaxing completely.

Take another deep breath and let go of all thoughts, all worries of the day.

As you allow your breathing to return to its normal rhythm, relax your body even more and feel a deep peace settling in your heart.

Feel your heart. Feel the peace, the stillness in your heart. And feel how your heart opens so sweetly, as it fills with Light.

Open your heart more and more, as your heart continues to fill with Light.

As your heart opens, feel how you connect so easily with the Divine Presence, that Great Ocean of Love, so spacious and luminous, so sweet and tender.

Feel the Love, feel the Light filling your whole body. All of your chakras, your aura, every cell in your body fill with the radiance of the Love, the beauty of the Light.

Now, feel how a sphere of Light is forming around your aura. The angels and other beings of Light bring more Light to your sphere until it is a radiant, luminous sphere all around you. This sphere of Light protects you completely.

Now, have the intention of going to the Temple of Light, where the essence of pure Love exists in all of its purity. Here,

Archangel Gabriel, the angels, archangels and other beings of Light will help you with this work of Light.

Feel your heart opening and filling with Love. Pause for a few moments while your whole being fills with Love.

Now your heart is open, beautiful and luminous. You are connected with all that is Love, with all that is Light. Your heart is connected to the Love of the Divine Presence and you feel this Ocean of Love filling your whole being. Your heart glows with Love.

Feel how your heart fills with even more Love and it opens completely to the Love. Your heart now radiates this Love to everything and everyone in existence.

Have the intention now of radiating this Love to the whole Earth and to all of her inhabitants: to all the animals, minerals, plants, human beings. To all of the natural world; to the devas and all of the nature spirits; to everyone and everything.

Feel the gratitude of the Earth and of the entire natural world as you radiate this Love.

Feel how the Divine Presence fills your heart with even more Love and through you, Divine Love radiates to all of nature.

Feel how this Love resonates with the Light that exists in each atom, each cell, in all of existence.

Feel how the Love resonates with your whole being and with the Earth's whole being. You are One with All that Is.

You are an open heart, connected to the totality of Love.

Allow this Love to flow through you, radiating in all directions, so luminous and sweet.

Expand your heart until nothing else exists, but the luminous purity of Love.

Dissolve, dissolve completely in the Love. You and the Love are ONE. You are One with the whole Earth and with all of nature.

Enjoy this oneness for as long as you wish.

When you are ready to return from this meditation, thank Archangel Gabriel, the devas and all the other beings of Light who assisted you.

Return slowly and gently from the Temple of Light, your heart filled with gratitude for all the blessings received.

Appendix II

Resources

I. Enlightened Spaces: Creating Your Sacred Space
www.espaciosiluminados.com
787.646.3591

For deep energy clearing, including curing geopathic stress, and the transformation of your home into a sacred space, contact Vanessa Arroyo or Rafael Rivera of Enlightened Spaces. They are the only space consultants certified by Paramita Path for this work of Light. They are also the only teachers certified to offer advanced Paramita Path workshops on this topic. The work can be done in person or distantly. For more detailed information about Enlightened Spaces, please visit their website.

II. Ezencia: Aromatherapy for the Spirit
www.ezencia.com
310.339.7952

Ezencia products are created with pure, organic essential oils in the presence of the Light. The blend for each scent is made with the sacred intention to fulfill its spiritual purpose. Yanira de Posson is the only aromatherapy practitioner certified by Paramita Path. Below are descriptions of the different blends available in room mists and bath salts.

Bliss

This blend opens the heart to universal joy. It lightens the density of the mind, bringing laughter and the radiance of the Light to your life. It assists you in reaching the angelic realms for guidance and help. This blend contains a frequency that allows you to let go of your fears, obsessions and judgment. It brings harmony, optimism and Light into your day. It lifts sadness from your life and opens your heart to the blessings of the Creator.

Serenity

This blend soothes the spirit, bringing harmony and peace. It fills the mind with silence and brings stillness to the heart. From the quiet space offered, you can listen to your Higher Self and tap into the wisdom of your heart. It encourages solace, tranquility and comfort. Depression and any deep sadness are washed away gently by the serene frequency of this blend. Love in all its manifestations is awakened by this fragrance and it brings the gift of grace to your life.

Enlightenment

This blend is for serious spiritual practitioners. It balances and harmonizes your energy channels to open your perception to subtle energies and to the higher realms. It increases your frequencies and opens your energy bodies to the Light. The blend purifies and cleanses so you can bring more Light to you. It awakens the heart and brings to your life the tolerance and understanding of unconditional love and compassion. It brings clarity of vision and assists you in realizing who you really are and attaining a sense of oneness with All-That-Is. This fragrance allows you to walk in the Light.

Surrender

This blend is also for serious spiritual practitioners and is a perfect complement to your meditation practice. It deepens your meditations, opens your heart and allows you to feel the joy of the Creator's Love. The blend assists you in dissolving in the Light of this Love. It brings to you the radiance of the heavens and creates a shift in your spirit that allows you to awaken to the Truth of who you are. It opens you to the guidance of the higher realms and allows your communication with the Creator to arise from your heart. All these transformations allow you to surrender completely to the Creator and fulfill your mission in this life.

Release

This combination of essential oils helps you to let go of attachments that you may need to release. It assists you in freeing ourselves from everything that is not Love in your life. Every time you meditate or pray with the intention of releasing attachments, you can use this scent to stimulate the energies of detachment in your physical, mental, emotional and spiritual bodies and gently dissolve the ties, hooks, cords or unnecessary desires and obsessions that don't allow you to surrender completely to the Love of the Creator and that are obstacles to your enlightenment.

Realm of Light

This sublime blend helps you to connect with the higher beings of Light, including angels, archangels, the great spiritual masters and other beings of Light for guidance, spiritual information and to help you raise your vibrations. This essence contains a very high frequency of Light and can transport you easily into the Kingdom of Light, helping you realize that you are part of that Light. It also helps you to receive divine messages in your dreams and meditations when you spray your space with this essence before bedtime or before meditating.

Room Clearing

This blend has the frequency of a protective spirit. Use it to protect, defend and clear all negativity in different spaces, (such as in a home, office, car, etc). This unique blend has very powerful components to cleanse and purify spaces. It calls to you the forces of protection (Archangel Michael and his angelic army) to help you in protecting yourself and your surroundings. It offers a protective shield that prevents negative energies and negative thoughts from contaminating your meditations and connections with the higher realms. It clears heart wounds and the scars you may have carried in your hearts for many lifetimes. It allows you to clear all negative thoughts, let go of attachments and forgive. This blend clears your path so you may move ahead with the Light unencumbered by the baggage of negativity.

Appendix III

The Paramita Path

The Paramita Path is a nonprofit society dedicated to spiritual healing and spiritual evolution based on divine Love. Through workshops, meditations and practice; the Paramita Path assists you in attaining an experience of unconditional love that can transform your life. The teachings of the Paramita Path guide you to open your heart to the Light of God-consciousness. This expansion is possible through the experience of Love in an activated spiritual heart.

The universal teachings of the Paramita Path empowers us to effect a transformation within that brings peace, harmony and love to the world around us. Our online meditations, workshops and practice allow for participation from anywhere in the world.

Paramita Path Centers
United States of America
Paramita Path Center Chapel Hill, NC
Telephone: 9119 338-2723
mail@paramitapath.org
www.paramitapath.org

Puerto Rico

Centro de Sendero Paramita
San Juan, Puerto Rico
Telephone: 787 646-3591
info@senderoparamita.org
www.senderoparamita.org

Spain

Paramita Path at La Calma
Wellness Center La Calma
Ribadesella, Asturias, Spain
Telephone: +34 985 861 804
info@la-calma.es www.la-calma.es

Paramita Path Workshops

The Paramita Path offers the following workshops:

Paramita Path Foundation

In this introductory weekend workshop, you are initiated into a path of spiritual healing and spiritual evolution. You open to the Light for self-healing, to heal others and for spiritual growth. Your Kundalini is activated and awakened and you are attuned to elemental energies for further healing and spiritual development. You become conscious of the Divine Presence within you and you connect, through your heart, to Divine Love and Light. You learn advanced meditations to attain God-consciousness. You learn a process to fill yourself with Divine Light and radiate it to others. You become a beacon of Light in the world.

You receive specific teachings regarding the Paramitas, the path to enlightenment based on unconditional love and compassion. The Paramitas are ancient principles that help you to live your life with love and kindness so that you can easily follow the Bodhisattva Path. The Bodhisattva is that kind and loving being who aspires to enlightenment not only for her/himself, but for all sentient beings.

Paramita Path Expansion

In this one-day workshop, you learn practices and meditations to assist you in opening your heart completely, attain conscious of your Oneness with the Divine Presence and advance on the journey that leads to enlightenment following the Bodhisattva Path. You learn to radiate unconditional love more effectively and to be a true beacon of Love and Light at all times. The attunements allow you to access the Sacred Space of your heart and listen to its infinite wisdom. You connect fully to Divine Love and Light and feel the joy of that connection. You learn to release attachments and begin working on the dissolution of your ego. You complete training in the Paramitas.

Once you have taken Paramita Path Foundation and Expansion workshops, you are ready for additional spiritual work. The following workshops will assist you in your spiritual journey.

Healing Your Karma with the New Light

You learn a powerful process that will assist you in removing karmic obstacles that prevent the full flowering of your spirit as your soul regains the absolute purity of the Light.

You receive a unique attunement that assists you in connecting with the Angels of Karma. This process will initiate changes in every aspect of your life as the karmic causes of illness, difficult situations, challenging relationships and personality issues are healed.

Awakening Your Heart

In this workshop you activate, open and awaken your heart for accelerated spiritual growth. Through special attunements, meditations and practices that are specifically designed, you can open your heart completely, connect with your soul and spirit and enter more fully into your path of enlightenment.

You learn a beautiful process to ask your heart for guidance. You learn to radiate unconditional love more effectively and to be a true beacon of Love and Light. As you open your heart and access the sacred space of your heart you can listen to the infinite wisdom of your True Self while you connect completely with the Creator's Heart. This places you firmly on a path leading to enlightenment through Divine Love and unconditional love toward other beings.

You learn practices to free yourself from the attachments that are an obstacle to opening your heart. You also attain a deep understanding of what your ego consists of and why it is necessary to dissolve it. You learn to radiate unconditional love to any situation or person and to change your reality by working with the Light in your heart.

At this advanced level you begin to remember who you truly are and to understand that your true identity dwells beyond your personal, physical identity. At this level of Light, you may acquire the consciousness of the divine being of Light that you are. Besides the material described above, spiritual teachings are included in this workshop that are only transmitted orally.

Creating Your Sacred Space I

In this workshop you learn to identify and remove negative energies from your home and workplace and fill them with Light. Using simple exercises and a variety of practices, you can transform your space into a beacon of Light that affects the outside world. You learn to distinguish between a variety of negative energies and learn effective techniques to clear each of these. You discover how to bring harmony to your living and work spaces. You also learn a spiritual technique to cure geopathic stress. This results in the healing and balancing of your space. You learn a beautiful process to transform your home into a sacred space dedicated to the Light. By following the methods discussed in the workshop, your space can become an oasis of radiant light bringing harmony, comfort and serenity to all who live there and to your environment.

Creating Your Sacred Space II

In this workshop, you learn advanced techniques that will allow you to do energy clearing of spaces and geopathic stress curing for other persons and distantly. The advanced techniques include the use of maps and architectural plans in the diagnostic and clearing processes. Also included are processes to identify and clear deep-rooted energies that require special techniques for their removal.

The Journey of Your Soul

In all your reincarnations you have lived the experiences that have helped you grow spiritually. You may have wondered:

"What has happened in past lives?" "What happens between reincarnations?" "What are the lessons I came to learn in my present life?" "How did the cycle of reincarnation begin?" "Why did we separate from the Creator?" In this workshop you will learn many of the mysteries of your soul's progress and master techniques to find answers to specific questions regarding the path of your soul. Through meditations, practices and regressions you will gain soul consciousness and attain a deeper understanding of why you are here.

About the Author

Renowned mystic, spiritual teacher and author Alba Ambert pioneered *Your Sacred Space*, a unique system to bring Light into spaces. As a result of profound mystical experiences, she received the Paramita Path system of spiritual healing and spiritual evolution as well as the spiritual practice of illuminating both public and private spaces. For many years she has been committed to facilitating the presence of the sacred in our lives. For this purpose, she founded the Paramita Path, a non-profit organization. Her workshops in Europe, the Caribbean and the United States have focused on the many aspects of practical spirituality. She is the author of *The Seven Powers of Spiritual Evolution*, *A Path of Light*, *Your Sacred Apothecary* and *Your Sacred Healing*. She received a doctoral degree in psycholinguistics from Harvard University.

For more detailed information on the Paramita Path, please visit:

www.paramitapath.org